THE PROFIT POTENTIAL

Previous Works by C.J. McNair

Benchmarking: Tool for Continuous Improvement with K. Leibfried. Essex Junction, VT: Oliver Wight Publishing/Omneo, 1992.

Beyond the Bottom Line: Measuring World Class Performance with W. Mosconi, and T. Norris. Homewood, IL: Business One Irwin, 1988.

Crossroads: A JIT Success Story with R. Stasey. Homewood, IL: Business One Irwin, 1990.

Meeting the Technology Challenge: Cost Accounting in a JIT Environment with W. Mosconi, and T. Norris. Montvale, NJ: Institute of Management Accountants, 1987.

World Class Accounting and Finance. Homewood, IL: Business One Irwin, 1993. This book has been adopted as the textbook for undergraduate management accounting at Babson College and was awarded the "Outstanding Academic Book" award for 1993 by *Choice Magazine*.

THE PROFIT POTENTIAL

TAKING HIGH PERFORMANCE TO THE BOTTOM LINE

Dr. C.J. McNair, CMA

omneo

AN IMPRINT OF THE OLIVER WIGHT PUBLICATIONS, INC.

85 Allen Martin Drive

Essex Junction, Vermont 05452

Oliver Wight Publications books may be purchased for educational,
business, or sales promotional use. For information, please call
or write: Special Sales Department, Oliver Wight Publications,
Inc., 85 Allen Martin Drive, Essex Junction, VT 05452.
Telephone: (800) 343-0625 or (802) 878-8161; FAX: (802) 878-3384.

Library of Congress Catalog Card Number: 94-076396

ISBN: 0-939246-66-X

Printed on acid-free paper.

Text design by Irving Perkins Associates

Manufactured in the United States of America.
2 4 6 8 10 9 7 5 3 1

To the memory of my parents, who taught me that common sense is the only sense that matters.

Contents

List of Figures and Tables

Figures

Tables

Acknowledgments

The ideas in this book have come from countless discussions, plant tours, company visits, meetings, presentations, and quiet talks that often lasted late into the night. Understanding waste and its effect on organizations is a journey that has been helped by each of these talks, every experience, and every thought that others have shared with me.

To thank each one of those who helped me over the years would be difficult. But you know what you have said and where your ideas appear, blended with the "CJisms" that inevitably pop up. Thanks to each of you for helping me learn to see the world a bit differently.

Some people have gone beyond the call of duty in supporting the development of this book. First, Jim Childs helped me persist at writing down these thoughts. Without him, I doubt the book would have been written. George put up with my "writer's tantrums," the frustrations, and the lost hours. I can never repay him for his patience or support. Jason, once again, had to wait in line for a few hours on the golf course with Mom. This time he even helped the project along—it was one way to squeeze in a few hours of golf before the snow flies.

I also would like to thank Gordon Shillinglaw for pointing me to management accounting so many years ago; Mike Gleason, who got my feet wet in the field; Richard Vangermeersch, who helped me learn so much about the history of waste measurements and capacity; and finally, Sandy Teixeira, who always seems to be there when I need her. A special thanks goes to Richard Lynch and Kelvin Cross, who first convinced me that waste was different than cost. Finally, to every manager who has shared their thoughts and opened their organization to me, thank you. Without your insights and openness none of this would have been possible.

Introduction

If we use nothing at all, is not then the waste total?

HENRY FORD
Today and Tomorrow (1926, p. 92)

A sustainable competitive advantage is the result of meeting or exceeding customer requirements. A customer pays for the perceived value of a good or service and not for its "cost." Relying on cost-plus pricing approaches to ensure long-term profits is akin to relying on a fairy godmother to make all your dreams come true. Faith may seem to work in the short run, but in the long run there is no magical way to avoid life's realities: prices are set by the market.

The market price is a hard, unbending cap on the amount of money a company can make by selling a good or a service. Within this constraint, management has the freedom to choose from a wide variety of structures, strategies, and management techniques. The goal pursued by management is clear: minimize total costs and maximize profits by meeting or exceeding customer requirements.

The lessons of the 1980s and 1990s have been hard ones for companies to learn. Focused on improving efficiencies and eliminating inefficiencies, companies have forgotten to ask the one vital question for their future: Are we doing the right things? In trying to solve the profitability puzzle, companies have often failed to examine what they are doing first. Effectiveness, which comes from recognizing and eliminating waste, is the key to sustainable growth.

In reality, there are three pieces to the puzzle management is trying to solve: *cost, waste,* and *profit.* Cost is the economic value of the resources a company uses in creating value for its customers: it is the total of all the activities the customer is willing to pay for. Market price less these *value-adding costs* is a company's profit *potential* on the good or service. Customers are willing to provide management with this potential profit.

The difference between the profit the customer is willing to provide and the actual profitability of a company is where waste has its impact. Waste, which is the economic value of all of the activities that a customer *is not* willing to pay for, comes out of potential profits. Since it is *non-value-adding* in the customer's eyes, waste is not going to be factored into the market price. High levels of waste, combined with a cost-plus pricing approach, can lead to a competitive nightmare as sales plummet, profits disappear, and unpaid bills stack up.

Managing a company out of a decline requires creativity and a focus on eliminating waste. The power of this approach can be seen in company after company. Motorola, Xerox, Harley-Davidson, and Bose Corporation are all known as effective competitors in the global marketplace. Each of these companies pursues the continuous elimination of waste (non-value-added work) from their ongoing operations. Less waste means more profits. By learning to do existing work better and by eliminating activities the customer doesn't value, many American firms are on the road to building a sustainable competitive advantage.

Make Waste Visible

Waste squeezes out the profits of a firm. Only by making waste visible, and by actively working to eliminate it, can a company gain long-term control over its profits. The result of hiding waste, of spreading it over marketable units of product or service, is that it effectively disappears from view. Hiding waste ensues its unbridled growth.

The unbridled growth of waste is almost a natural outcome of success. When a company is in its growth stage, it cannot add resources fast enough to meet demand. Trying to catch up, management adds more and more resources, even as the market begins to mature. The total amount of added cost, spread out over an increasing volume of products, seems unimportant. Only when the company hits maturity does the high cost of unbridled growth hit home. By then, so much waste is hidden in the measurements, management, and processes used to deliver products and services to customers that it is virtually impossible to uncover.

The only way to turn around this downward spiral of increasing waste and evaporating profits is to measure, and then eliminate, waste throughout the organization. But few companies actually do measure waste. Why? Because waste is what we have done wrong. Measurements seldom focus on what we do wrong, and when they do, it is in a piecemeal fashion.

The only reliable way to affect behavior is to measure it, and to use these measures to reward individuals for their efforts. If the key to long-term sustainable growth is the continuous elimination of waste, the entire measurement process has to focus on waste. Waste has to be weighed, labeled, displayed, and managed to be permanently eliminated. Total quality management (TQM) provides a company with many of the metrics needed to track waste on the plant floor, but the key yardstick used to measure company performance is not as supportive. The accounting system provides no information on waste. It records "cost," a number that blends the good (value-adding work) with the bad (non-value-adding activities).

Undoing the damage done by allocations and poor knowledge of the underlying dynamics of value creation will require a sustained effort by companies to honestly record, monitor, and eliminate waste. This change starts with recognizing that every resource has the capability to create value. Value-creating potential—not historical cost—is the baseline measurement for the economic worth of an asset. It is this basic value-creating potential that needs to be managed and optimized. While most managers would agree with this statement, the mechanics of creating a value-focused accounting process are not as easily agreed upon.

The current move to "reengineer" corporations is one way companies are trying to drive value creation into every process and activity they undertake. But reengineering is a "re." "Re's," as described in the pages that follow, are the actions taken to correct previous mistakes. To avoid being merely a "re," reengineering efforts need to highlight the amount of waste that is embedded in an organization—in its assumptions and in its practices. Are the activities being performed the ones the customer is willing to pay for? If downsizing takes place, will the company lose a core competency? Do top-down cost-reduction drives, under whatever name, really ensure that waste is eliminated and long-term sustainable profits are guaranteed?

Management will get the type of behavior it measures and rewards. If management believes that it has to eliminate fat and waste from the organization, it needs new measurements that accurately track existing waste levels and pinpoint areas where improvement will result in increased long-term profitability. These measures are not an option; they are the key to gaining a sustainable competitive advantage in the global market.

Waste-based measurement systems don't look, act, or feel like traditional accounting measures. Instead, they reflect the realities of organizational life. If $1 million in resources is needed to process customer complaints, then $1 million of waste needs to be recorded and discussed. The merging of these non-value-adding costs with other resource costs hides the true profit potential of a company. Measuring these non-value-adding costs, thereby making them visible, is the key to eliminating them.

This is Japan's secret. Simply, they have a deep respect for the learning that comes from recognizing, studying, and fixing mistakes. Mistakes are waste. Waste robs a company of its profit-creating potential if and only if it is not learned from. To learn from mistakes, a company needs a way to discuss them and see their effects in terms of dollars of wasted resources. This lesson must be learned by Western companies and their managers if a sustainable competitive advantage is to be gained.

A Personal Note

The role of waste in defining a company's profitability and the need to measure this vital area of company performance became clear to me as I studied the differences between old and new methods of managing factories and offices. What separated these new techniques from their older cousins was the way they directed everyone's attention to the waste embedded in the way an organization did its work. The common denominator in all of these continuous-improvement models was waste.

The troubling issue, though, was the lack of measurements for recording current levels of waste or for preventing new waste in the future. The accounting numbers I had learned so well in earlier parts of my life did not provide any insight into waste. They were driven by a concern to balance the ledger. Accounting relied on average costs, and I knew that "average" simply wasn't good enough for the future.

Understanding waste and its impact on a company's health became a passion for me. Everywhere I went, I saw good companies assuming that large levels of waste were inevitable. I saw good people doing work they knew was non-value-adding but having no recourse but to keep on doing the work they were told to do. I saw company after company struggling to implement the newest management fad to bandage hemorrhages of waste that were bleeding them dry. Unable to see, or accurately measure, the root cause of their declining profitability—waste—these good companies continued to struggle. Some were successful, but all too many were unsuccessful in their battle against the weight of waste that was dragging them down.

Once the role of waste became clear to me, I knew it had to be measured. The profit bandits had to be made visible so that people could act on the sources of waste. I had to find a way to show people that waste was all around them—to focus their attention on eliminating waste from their organizations. That goal led to this book and to the ideas and measures that follow. Making waste visible is a journey that has just begun for me. It is one that will take a lifetime to complete.

THE PROFIT
POTENTIAL

CHAPTER 1

The Profit Potential

A man cannot be paid much for producing something which is wasted.

HENRY FORD
Today and Tomorrow (1926, p. 93)

You've often heard the phrase "one person's junk is another person's treasure." Behind this simple statement is the notion of perspective—the unique set of values, beliefs, experiences, and knowledge that shapes what people see when they look at the world around them. These perspectives are molded by family and friends, education, work, and the culture at large. In the business world, numbers play a major role in shaping these perspectives. Ideas that can be expressed in terms of numbers—profit and loss, revenues, and costs—seem more real, more manageable, and more important than those simply described with words.

Given the key role played by numbers in managing Western businesses, it is critical that these numbers reflect reality, that they measure the "right" things. What are the "right" things? Most managers say they want to know the real cost of making a product or supplying a service: What do they make a profit on and why? Common belief is that this "real" cost is the foundation for sound business decisions.

3

What is cost? For businesspeople, *cost* is the economic value of the resources used to do the work required to meet customer expectations. It includes every hour of labor, every dollar of materials, and every indirect expense that is *caused by* the decision to make the products or provide the services a customer requests. If these caused costs are kept low enough, a company can expect a profit from its activities.

When a company decides it wants to improve its profits, it focuses traditionally either on increasing sales or reducing its costs. Yet today company after company is finding that the real key to increasing profits is not to sell more or to implement across-the-board cost-reduction mandates, but rather to shift its perspective. This shift begins with the recognition that all costs are not equal. Some "costs" provide value to the customer; others don't. Companies are redefining themselves around one simple concept: *Eliminate waste.*

Waste? As illogical as it sounds, the key to unleashing a company's *profit potential* is the clear, honest, and accurate recognition and elimination of waste, anywhere it occurs in the organization. *Kaizen,* or the process of *continuous improvement through the elimination of waste,* is the essence of the revolution that is changing the way companies are managed today. Built from distinctly American roots, the principles of kaizen reflect Henry Ford's vision and unending quest to make his automobiles better, faster, and cheaper than the competition's. Ford accomplished this goal by removing waste from the manufacturing process. He understood that knowing what it costs, on average, to make a product or provide a service didn't mean that the customer would be willing to reimburse a company for its expense; value is the currency of the global marketplace.

At Ford Motor Company, the lessons of its founder are reshaping its future. If market results are any gauge of success, Ford appears to be on the right track. It has edged out domestic and foreign competitors to become one of the top-selling car and truck producers in the United States. This success isn't the result of any specific management tool, such as total quality management, but rather of a single-minded focus on eliminating waste from the manufacturing process. If, for instance, a capital asset is purchased because it will save twenty-five cents in production cost, the standards used to track the production process are ramped down by twenty-five cents the day the new machine is put on line. At Ford, managers know that trimming waste and inefficiency from all facets of the business isn't a slogan: it is reality, enforced through numbers that are finely tuned to reflect actual events on the shop floor.

As shown by Ford, the key to gaining a sustainable competitive advantage begins with understanding how and where waste is being built into the very fabric of the process, management techniques, and measurements used within a company. The goal, or driving force, behind this approach is a simple belief:

> *A company has to recognize, measure, and eliminate waste if it is to achieve its profit potential.*

In the numbers-driven world of Western management, the invisible cancer of unmeasured and uncontrolled waste threatens the existence of businesses, large and small. Only by clearly measuring, reporting, and intensely working to eliminate waste can the competitive battle be won.

THE PROFIT POTENTIAL

> *I don't want to do business with those who don't make a profit, because they can't give the best service.*
>
> LEE BRISTOL (3)[1]

The key to long-term growth is a company's profit potential—or its *ability to earn reasonable profits on its current and future sales to customers.* Profit is what is left over after all the costs of doing business are paid; it is the residual in the business equation that spells the difference between success and failure in the competitive global economy. There are very few people, either in or out of business, who don't realize that a company has to be profitable to survive, but when a company slips "into the red," what can it do?

Clearly, many companies have tried to raise prices to recover lost profits, but it takes only a bit of economics to point out the fallacy of this approach. In fact, unless a company is in the enviable position of being a monopolistic supplier of goods or services, raising prices will mean simply that more and more of the company's sales go to a competitor. This is the iron law of supply and demand that lies at the heart of a customer-driven economy.

In reality, most companies don't have the power to set the prices for their goods and services unfettered from the customer's view of the *value* those goods and services represent. Customers are, in fact, paying a company for a *value-adding core of activities* (see Figure 1.1). Market price, set by customers based on this perceived value, places a defined outer boundary around the potential revenues and profits a company can earn.

Looking further at Figure 1.1, the real challenge facing a company becomes clear. Market price is the limit—the cap on what can be charged for a good or service. The value-added core of activities is the minimal amount of work that can be done to meet customer expectations and earn the desired market price. In between the market price and the cost of the resources consumed to perform the core activities lies the *profit zone*. If a company did only work the customer valued and used no other resources at all, the entire difference between the market price for its goods and services and the value-adding cost required to provide them would drop to the "bottom line" as profits. What level of profits could a company expect if it were this efficient? While the exact percentage would likely vary by industry, somewhere between 20 and 40 percent would be a reasonable profit.

Impossible? Not really. In fact, the best companies in the world do consistently earn between 20 to 40 percent profit before taxes and reinvestments are considered. Toyota, Motorola, and Hewlett-Packard, for instance, use a market-driven approach, called *target costing*[2] to ensure that desired profit levels are built into a product before the first unit is even produced. Target costing identifies excess

FIGURE 1.1 THE PROFIT POTENTIAL

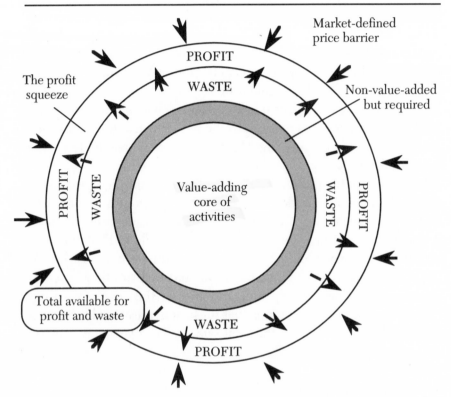

cost—waste—that has to be taken out of a product before it can achieve its profit potential.

Of course, companies do a lot of work that a customer may not value but that is a necessary part of staying in business. For instance, a customer may not place any value on closing the company's books, issuing financial statements, or completing tax forms, but this work has to be done. This *non-value-added but required* (NVA-R) work eats away at the potential profits of the firm but cannot be avoided.

Some economists, most notably Oliver Williamson,[3] suggest that these non-value-added but required activities are part of the equation customers use in reaching a decision on a fair price. The logic behind Williamson's work is simple: customers are paying a company to perform the various market transactions (such as organizing production, pulling together materials from many different sources, and so on) that they would have to do if they decided to do the work on their own. Much like the fee paid to a contractor who organizes the building of a house, the management of a company is allowed a certain amount of money to cover non-value-added but required activities. The alternative for the customer would be a return to the craft society of the 1700s, where gathering together the goods needed to survive was a full-time job.

If we look at the profit picture in Figure 1.1 in this light, we can see that these non-value-added but required activities consume a layer of resources in a company, represented by a dark band within the profit potential circle. What percentage of costs is allowed? While, once again, the answer would be different for different industries (for instance, industries with high pollution-control restrictions would be given a higher premium by the customer for this regulatory-driven work), a good rule of thumb is that these activities should represent about 10 to 20 percent of the total sales dollar a company receives. Where does that leave us?

$$\frac{\text{Market}}{\text{price}} - \frac{\text{Cost of resources for}}{\text{the value-added core}} = \frac{\text{Profit potential}}{\text{or, in numbers:}}$$

$$1.00 - 60\% = 40\%$$

Factoring in the cost of non-value-added but required (NVA-R) work, we see

$$\frac{\text{Profit}}{\text{potential}} - \frac{\text{Cost of resources}}{\text{for NVA-R work}} = \frac{\text{Available profit}}{\text{or, in numbers:}}$$

$$40\% - 10\% = 30\%$$

At least 30 percent of every sales dollar is the potential profit for every sale made by a company! While one could quibble, perhaps, that this should be only 25 percent, the message is clear: a reasonable, sustainable profit level is built into the market's price for a good or a service.

Returning to the concept of the profit potential, then, it is clear that a company can attain consistently high profitability levels. If it doesn't, is it because of poor management or poor products? Not really. *The real villain is waste: companies throw away their profits through unmeasured and uncontrolled waste.* In fact, the band of potential profits is shared by profit and by waste. If waste grows unabated, it simply squeezes the profits, and life, out of the firm. It is this fact, and this fact alone, that makes it essential that waste be measured, reported, controlled, and eliminated: it is stealing the profits that are essential to long-term survival.

THE PROFIT BANDITS

The ideal is to have nothing to salvage.

HENRY FORD
Today and Tomorrow (1926, p. 94)

Waste, wherever it occurs in the organization, robs a company of its profits and its future. This was clearly understood by Henry Ford and led to the building of the River Rouge facility, which used intensive vertical integration. It is common sense that waste is undesirable. As Benjamin Franklin stated in *Poor Richard's Almanack*, "Waste not, want not." Why isn't this commonsense reality visible in Western businesses? As the discussion below reveals, waste is averaged into a company's standard cost, built into its engineered estimates, and hidden in so-called assets such as inventory. Waste is hidden from view by the measurements and methods used to manage a company. If anyone is to blame for this sad state of affairs, it is the people who developed these methods, not those who trustingly use them. Hiding waste doesn't eliminate it, but it does make it invisible to the naked eye. What isn't seen can't be dealt with.

One of the best ways to understand how hidden waste eats into profits is to review some of the new management techniques that have helped Western companies regain lost competitive prowess (see Figure 1.2). While the techniques listed in this diagram are familiar to most businesspeople today, it is useful to look at each of these tools from the standpoint of the type of waste they target for elimination. That is their common element: each of these techniques brings the kaizen ideal to life by focusing on different aspects of the productive process. What are the types of waste—*the profit bandits*—targeted by these tools?

FIGURE 1.2 THE PROFIT BANDITS

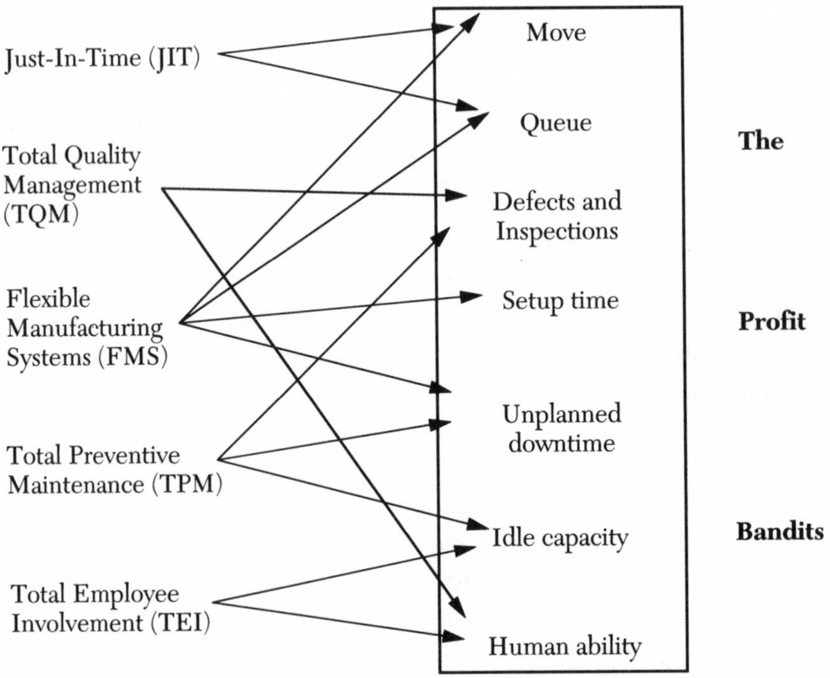

Hidden Sources of Waste

There are seven primary types of waste present in all organizations: move, queue, defects and inspections, setup time, unplanned downtime, idle capacity, and human ability. Some might argue that this sounds like a "manufacturing" list of ills, but whether a company moves product, paper, or ideas, each of these types of waste can occur. For instance, in most offices paperwork is done in batches because of the belief that doing similar work at one time is the most efficient way to operate (economies of scale). If a purchasing manager believes that it is most efficient to do all the ordering in the morning, material requisitions will sit at least one day before being worked on. That adds one full day of delay or lead time to the work being done for the customer—a day wasted that cannot be recovered. In fact, it would not be difficult to come up with a "back office" example for every type of waste in the "profit bandits" list. It is a universal set of ills.

At one major bank, a total quality management exercise revealed a form of waste that, in retrospect, was hard to believe. The bank decided to trace the work required to open a new customer account. As the process was documented, waste and inefficiency began to be exposed. One example of this waste appeared in the delivery of forms by the new accounts clerk to the data processing department. The clerk recorded key information about the new account on forms and assembled the completed packet in the order specified in her procedures manual. Once a day, these completed packets were carried down the hall to data processing, where they were date stamped and handed to an operator. The operator then unstapled each packet and rearranged the forms in the order required by the computer data input program. This "rework" was waste: there was no logic to it, it didn't add value to any part of the organization or to the service the customer received, yet it had been going on for as long as anyone could remember.

Was this bank poorly managed? No, in fact it is one of the best managed banks in the world. But practices that developed over time but were never questioned, let alone changed, had resulted in wasted time and effort. Did the workers care? Yes. In fact, there aren't many people who happily work all day to create waste—to see their efforts thrown away. When waste is visible, it is easy to get everyone focused on eliminating it. Changing processes is difficult only if the reasons for the change seem arbitrary—dictated by people who simply don't understand how things "really work around here." When the problem is revealed—when the waste can be seen—eliminating it is possible and probable.

Targeting the Profit Bandits

Some of the new management techniques that have been developed to deal with waste in business processes, procedures, products, and services include just-in-time manufacturing and purchasing (JIT), total quality management (TQM), flexible manufacturing systems (FMS), total preventive maintenance (TPM), and total employee involvement (TEI). Each of these tools targets one or more profit bandits (see Figure 1.2). For instance, TQM focuses on eliminating defects or errors from work. It also focuses on the "whole person" concept, attempting to eliminate the waste of human problem-solving ability by a company. TQM is a technique that is being used by companies in every industry, and every location, to turn performance around and increase the level of value delivered to customers. Improvement comes not from buying new machines but from eliminating waste.

The power of TQM in eliminating waste and improving performance is unquestioned by most companies today. As noted by one of the 1993 winners of the Malcolm Baldrige award, Joel Marvil of Ames Rubber,[4] "Non-TQM companies are not going to survive beyond the year 2000 or 2005. I would dearly love it if none of my competitors embraced total-quality. Unfortunately, not many of them are that dumb." TQM embodies the message that waste has to be eliminated everywhere it occurs and is seen by its proponents as essential to achieving a sustainable competitive position.

In a similar way, just-in-time methods (used by manufacturing, financial services, and many other industries) target for elimination the wasted resources caused by "move" and "queue" activities. While inventories do go down as a result of eliminating move and queue activities from the process, JIT does not focus on inventory: it focuses on eliminating the forms of waste that create the need for large levels of buffer inventories. According to many JIT proponents, simply moving machines out of functional departments into cells that correspond to the way a product is made yields 80 percent of the total performance improvement possible. Companies like Stanadyne Diesel, a revitalized New England manufacturer of diesel engine components, trace their turnarounds to the benefits of eliminating waste through JIT manufacturing.

The benefits of removing move and queue activities are not confined to manufacturing companies. Citibank has successfully used JIT concepts to revamp the back-office operations that handle millions of checks every day. Grouping all the activities, people, and machines that are needed to completely process a check has greatly reduced the throughput time and resources required to perform this essential task. Just-in-time concepts have a place in every organization.

Flexible manufacturing systems (FMS) have been defined in various ways by the trade press, but the definitions share the recognition that flexible production starts with eliminating the waste caused by setups. Setup time, move, idle capacity, and queue forms of waste are all reduced when FMS is put in place. The savings come from reducing setup times to their bare minimum, which triggers reductions in required buffer inventories while improving the throughput of materials through the factory. The goal—flexible production—is achieved by eliminating the sources of waste that block the path of materials through the plant. In similar ways, TPM and TEI target different profit bandits for elimination (unplanned downtime and the waste of human capability).

Removing Waste: Seeing is Believing?

The common element of these tools for improving a company's performance is their single-minded focus on identifying and eliminating the sources of waste in a company. Company after company has seen the benefits of these techniques, but in many cases these "improvements" don't show up in the bottom line. This confusing fact has led some critics to believe that each of these tools is simply a fad—that touted improvements are due to the Hawthorne effect.[5]

Another explanation of this apparent contradiction could and should be made, though. If managers on the plant floor and in the office actually can see the long-term improvement in the flow of work through the company when JIT concepts are put in place, how can the label "Hawthorne" be applied to these changes? These are not temporary improvements; examples of ongoing improvement that have persisted for five years or longer have been documented at companies like Hewlett-Packard, Xerox, Johnson & Johnson, Citibank, 3M, and Motorola. A solid list of top performers appears to be gaining long-term benefits from the changes made based on the new tools and these ideas contained in the kaizen message.

What sets these companies apart from those that appear to "fail" at gaining benefits from JIT, TQM, and their cousins? The one key difference that defines these companies is that they have made changes to their measurements and management techniques to honestly capture, report, and eliminate waste from their operations. For instance, when a JIT cell is put together in a factory, it effectively eliminates much of the move, queue, defect, and setup costs buried in the manufacturing process. At Motorola this effect is captured by measuring actual performance against a theoretical cell-capacity measure that allows no waste.

There is a catch to JIT, however, that Motorola's measurements reveal. When move, queue, and related forms of waste are eliminated, a new type of waste is created: idle capacity. If a cell is created, excess capacity is generated. Unless this idle capacity is filled with new production or eliminated, profits will not improve. Just exchanging one form of waste for another is not the goal. To really benefit from JIT, a company has to either reduce the total resources used, or run more volume through the system. Otherwise the changes simply create new forms of waste. Waste is waste, wherever it occurs. That is the lesson that Motorola has learned and built into the performance measurements it uses to evaluate its JIT cells.

Long-term, sustainable change has to be built into the performance measurement system used to manage a company. This change begins with clearly identifying where waste is and then actively working to eliminate it. Elimination does not mean shifting waste from one pocket to another—from move and queue to idle capacity. Eliminating waste means getting rid of it, either through better use of the resources at hand, reduction of the total resources needed to get a job done, or decreasing the level of investment (capacity) necessary to meet customer demand. Measuring and reporting waste is the missing link to sustainable growth through continuous improvement.

MEASURING WASTE TO IMPROVE PROFITS

We will use material more carefully if we think of it as labor.

HENRY FORD
Today and Tomorrow (1926, p. 92)

In essence, the message embedded in this book is a simple one: *Recognizing, measuring, and eliminating waste are the keys to a sustainable competitive advantage.* If waste is going to be eliminated, it first has to be defined, described, and made clearly visible to everyone, no matter where an individual works in the company. The basis for creating this new language of waste is the separation of value-added cost from its nemesis: waste. Throughout this book, these terms are used in precise ways, as defined here:

Value-adding cost (VAC)   The economic value of the minimal resources required to make products or deliver services to the customer.

Non-value-adding but required cost (NVA-R)   The economic value of the minimal resources required to sustain the organization.

Waste   Total cost less all value-adding cost and non-value-adding but required cost.

Profit   Total revenues minus total cost.

Profit potential   Total revenues minus value-adding cost and non-
value-adding but required cost.

Cost is what a customer is reimbursing a company for when it buys
goods and services. Value-added cost defines the boundaries on the
profit potential of a company and sets the limits on allowable waste.
Price less cost, defined in this way, is what is available to the company
for profits. Cost is based on the theoretical best a company can
deliver—the optimal mix of machines, people, and support services
used to create products and services the customer values.

What is waste? Waste is everything else. Waste is idle machines on
the plant floor, underutilized people, unneeded materials, and every
other form of excess spending that takes place. While it may not be a
comforting term, it is truthful, and it will get action. Isn't that the
purpose of language and information? It is time for everyone in the
private and public sectors to come clean—to publicly and honestly
recognize that there is a problem: waste. Waste has to be recognized,
measured, and eliminated.

Imagine the power that would be unleashed if every form of waste—
the lost profits—that a company has buried in its structures and processes were revealed. The initial message might be hard to accept, but
if the right focus is given to this information—that waste is simply
another way to view untapped profit potential in a company—a strong
positive force for future growth and competitive viability could be
unleashed. If the enemy can be seen, it can be conquered. Revealing
the monster called waste in all of its various forms is the starting point
in a journey that can help reshape the way we manage our companies
and our country (see Figure 1.3). Profits are buried in the unseen layers
of waste—the trash of economic life—that surround every organization, every manager, every activity the company performs.

FIGURE 1.3 PUTTING WASTE WHERE IT BELONGS

Layers of Hidden Waste

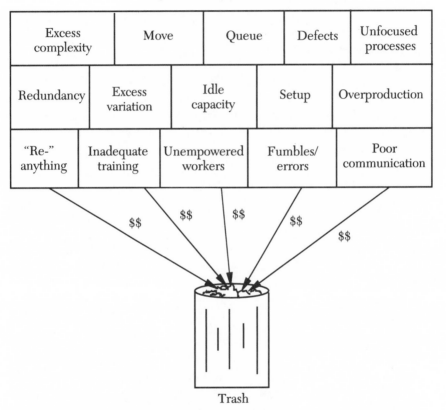

Excess complexity	Move	Queue	Defects	Unfocused processes
Redundancy	Excess variation	Idle capacity	Setup	Overproduction
"Re-" anything	Inadequate training	Unempowered workers	Fumbles/ errors	Poor communication

Trash

Take out the trash . . . and what you have left is your profit potential.

As the story of waste and its sources unfolds in the following pages, you will learn about the current myths that shape the world of business. You will explore the myths and errors embedded in traditional financial measurements, as well as the myths tied to the economies-of-scale theory and other assumptions that underlie most Western management techniques. The objective is not to destroy the structure of business and the measurements it currently relies on, but to pull away the veil that hides the waste that slowly eats away profits until survival itself becomes questionable for many companies. The goal is to create a new awareness of waste and its hiding places so that a company's profit potential can become its reality.

Knowledge is the only instrument of production that is not subject to diminishing returns.

JOHN MAURICE CLARK (2)

CHAPTER 2

Waste Versus Cost: Defining the Territory

Habit and routine have an unbelievable power to waste and destroy.

HENRI DE LUBAC
Paradoxes (1)

Day-to-day life in a company consists of habits and routines that are reinforced by numbers and reward systems. The driving force behind these habits—to maximize profits and sustainable growth—is unquestioned. The "how" that goes into reaching preset goals is normally left to the individuals who perform the activities that make up the company's *value chain*. Whether clearly spelled out through process analysis or simply "understood" but invisible, the value chain, or sequence of activities done to fill an order, is an intricate part of meeting or exceeding customer requirements. Each of these activities consumes some of the organization's scarce resources, generating either profit or waste. Separating the "good" activities (value creating) from the "bad" (waste creating) does not appear to be a simple task.

Or is it? It is an admittedly daunting task to list every activity a company performs on a daily basis, to figure out exactly how many resources are consumed every time that segment of work is completed, to develop every possible path an order for a product or service could follow through the organization, or to identify every possible combination of materials, labor, machines, and other resources it uses to deliver its wide variety of products and services to customers. Just making the list would consume large amounts of resources. And the value-added of doing the analysis and making the lists would itself be questionable. Would the customer care? Would the customer benefit? Probably not. Clearly, writing down everything a company does and how it affects every resource is an impossible task or at least one that would take a very long time to complete.

Then how can "good" versus "bad" activities be identified? Don't we need this detailed understanding before we can move forward on the path to continuous improvement? The answer is, quite simply, no. Why? Perhaps the best way to answer this question is to reexamine what we're trying to do and the assumptions we're using to guide our thoughts.

A FOCUS ON THE "WHOLE"

There can be little theory of any account unless it corroborate with the theory of the earth.

WALT WHITMAN (4)

In everyday life, we are becoming increasingly aware that our lives are intertwined with the world around us. If the rain forest is cut down in Brazil, the weather throughout the world is changed. If an animal species becomes extinct, it affects every other living thing on earth as this loss ripples across the food chain that knits together life on this planet. In other words, nature is constantly reminding us that every plant, animal, and rock on Earth is part of an interlocking, interreacting whole—a system.

When Parts Don't Matter

For many years, the theories and approaches developed by scientists and businesspeople to understand and "control" their world have been based on an assumption that is contrary to a belief in the systemic, interlocking nature of life. This assumption has shaped the basic education and views of Westerners, blinding them to many of the potential solutions and methods so natural to those from other parts of the world. What is this assumption? For a very long time, Westerners have felt that the best way to understand how something works is to break it down into its smallest parts—to dissect it. In other words, by breaking the "system" into smaller and smaller parts, you'll eventually reach the core—the basic building block that lies at its heart.

If we think about the logic behind this approach, we soon encounter some troubling issues. If you have to dissect an animal to understand what makes it function, what are you left with? A dead animal. The very essence of the life being sought slips through your fingers as you separate bone from tissue. At the end of the process, or *destructive test*, you have an inanimate object and a bit of knowledge about what stops its functioning. As the scientific argument goes, though, if you keep dissecting things long enough, you'll finally understand the system—the entire organism. But common sense says that this knowledge-gaining process seems flawed.

Using this analogy in a business setting, we might feel that the best way to find the essence of the value-creation process in an organization is to keep digging deeper and deeper into the detail of the work it does—its structure and basic processes. If you dissect it enough, you'll discover what makes that organization tick—how it functions. Or will you? You'll know a lot about the parts that make up the organization, but will you understand it? Can you, by completing a detailed record of every resource, every person, every machine, every office, and so on, know how that company functions or what makes it better at delivering value to its customers than its competitors are? Probably not. What would be missing are the culture, the interactions, the flows, and the mental models that guide action in the organization. Understanding the parts that make up the company does not really help you understand the whole.

Is understanding and improving an organization an art? Is it alchemy—a scientific experiment that cannot be controlled but that sometimes yields gold? If you believe (or assume) that the only way to really understand the organization is to understand its parts, then this is a logical conclusion. But what if you change your focus just a bit— and challenge the basic assumption about how to understand and manage an organization?

What would that change be? The simplest way to think about it is that you would view the organization as an entity—one where parts interact on an ongoing basis to create a whole that is greater than their sum. You would think of the organization as a *system*, not as a bunch of discrete activities, resources, or structures. What does this really mean? It means that we can't really understand all the complex interactions and processes that have developed over time to create an organization. But we can understand those events and practices that suck the lifeblood out of the organization and make the whole less than the sum of its parts (see Figure 2.1). By focusing on *waste*, the leakages from the system, we can improve an organization's perfor- mance without having to dig into every nook and cranny of its offices and factories.

Waste: Focusing on What Isn't Working

If we think of waste as the leakage that inhibits an organization from reaching its true value-creating potential, we begin to have a mental model, or approach, that focuses our attention on things that we can fix and have an immediate positive impact on the bottom line. Reflec- tive of Occam's Razor,[1] this single-minded focus on waste—the en- tropy or loss of value from the system—provides a simple, easily applied, and clearly defined basis for improvement. No one likes waste. Nature abhors waste. Systems that have excessive levels of waste perish. It's a natural phenomenon. Using waste as the starting

FIGURE 2.1 WHEN WASTE TAKES ITS TOLL

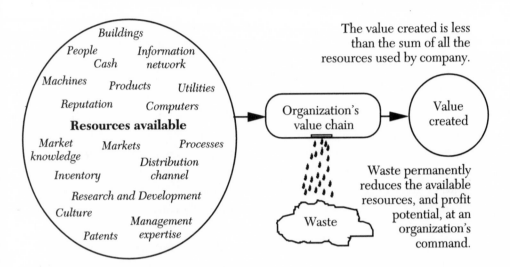

point provides us with a natural approach to thinking about the complex organizations that surround us in terms we can communicate, illustrate, and act upon.

To put these concepts to work, though, it is useful to classify the types of waste that may occur in an organization. This is because the type of action needed to eliminate waste differs based on the type of waste involved. Waste that is embedded in the structure of the organization is different from waste created by *how* its work is done. Structural waste is harder to see and eliminate than process-based waste.

Thinking about an organization, then, we know that it has a structure and that resources flow through this structure in the process of creating value. A simple analogy for an organization might be a garden hose. The hose itself is the structure that shapes or constrains the path that water will follow. But a hose is of little value unless water is coursing through it. The "system" used to water a lawn requires a structure (the hose) and a process or flow through that structure (the water). If you want to increase the amount of water that can be moved through this system, you can change the size of the hose (the structure) or turn up the water pressure (more flow). Waste in this setting would be a hose that is too large or too small for the amount of water you want to move, a leak in the hose, too much or too little water pressure, and so on. To improve the effectiveness of this water-delivery system, the simplest approach would be to stop all leaks—to eliminate waste.

In looking at larger systems and organizations, the basic features of structure and flow continue to provide a basis for understanding the system and how effectively it uses resources. This basic model provides a useful framework for categorizing the type of waste we may find in an organization into two basic groups: (1) waste driven by the design of the system (structural waste) and (2) waste created by how the system is used (process waste) (see Figure 2.2). Looking deeper into these two categories of waste provides some useful insights.

FIGURE 2.2 STRUCTURAL AND PROCESS-BASED WASTE

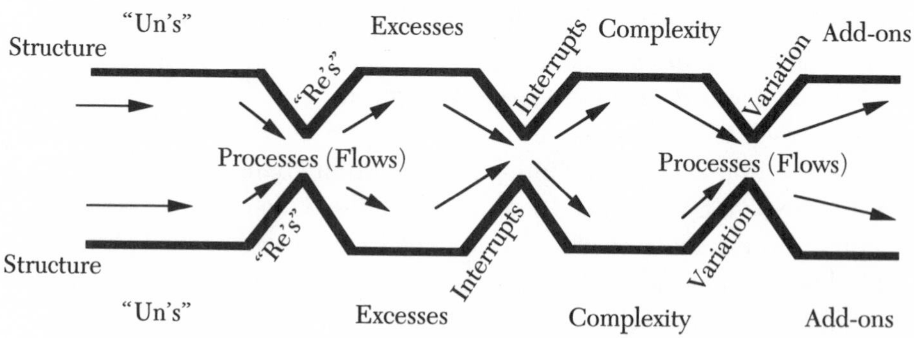

Structural waste restricts the growth of the total organization.

Process-based waste restricts the total amount of value the organization can create within its structural boundaries.

STRUCTURAL WASTE—OR DESIGNING
WASTE INTO OUR WORK

Destiny is not a matter of chance, it is a matter of choice.

CALDWELL VAN RODEN (6)

The way that a company is structured defines the type and amount of resources it will need. This *structure—or the number of plants, divisions, departments, or related "parts" it has, where they are located, and how they interact*—sets the stage for the value-creation process. And in the same way that the structure of the garden hose constrains the amount of water that can flow through it, the structure of an organization constrains the amount of work it can do in any defined period of time.

How can we apply the concept of cost and waste to the actual design of the organization? There are three basic ways that waste is built in, increasing total cost for operating the system and delivering goods and services:

- Excess capacity of the system in total, or of specific key resources;

- Inadequate development of the baseline capability of the people that interact within the system; and

- Unnecessary or excessive complexity in the structure and activities of the value chains that deliver specific goods and services to customers and markets.

A Problem of Excesses

Just as the design of a product locks in its cost, the design of an organization builds in a required amount of resources and effort for its functioning. Waste can also be designed into an organization. One of the clearest examples of this type of waste is visible at General Motors.[2] It is no secret that one of the major challenges facing General Motors today is excess capacity. The company was built on the premise that each new model or line of automobiles or components requires a new plant for its production. Rather than seeking economies of scale or redeploying its assets to produce new items, General Motors has simply added more resources—and, it seems, more waste—to its structure. In contrast, two companies that have taken a different approach to plant design are Ford Motor Company and Motorola.

At Ford Motor Company, new plants are not built unless the capacity of the entire system of plants has been exceeded. Production is moved from one plant to another based on projected demand versus plant capacity for output. The ability of this policy to minimize built-in or structural waste can be seen at the Twin Cities plant in Minneapolis–St. Paul. Since its construction in 1924, this plant has made a wide variety of products from Model Ts to tanks to Ranger trucks. In fact, a quick review of the models built each year is painted on one wall of the factory. What is striking is the diversity of products: it is unusual for a product to be made in the plant for more than one to three years. Yet the plant itself is little changed from the days of Henry Ford. True, a painting wing has been added, since Henry Ford's view that a customer can have any color as long as it is black is unacceptable to modern consumers. Except for minor changes to accommodate shifting consumer demands, the plant continues to turn out automobiles and trucks within the same factory walls Henry Ford designed and built.

At Motorola, a similar approach is taken to balancing the company's physical production capacity across the globe. Faced with rapidly changing product lines and market demands, Motorola is constantly reexamining and shifting its production of specific products around the globe to maximize its total output at minimum cost. The strategy being pursued reflects a single-minded focus on eliminating waste, including the waste created by idle capacity.

Waste Within the System or Plant

Ford and Motorola focus on minimizing wasted capacity across all of their potential production sites to improve profitability. But the waste that can be embedded in the structure of an organization can also be traced to its individual processes. One of the most poignant examples we have of this type of waste can be found in the book *The Goal*, a modern business classic.[3] In this book, a plant manager, Alex Rogo, learns to look at his organization through new eyes.

The driving theme behind Alex's learning process is that managing a complex system begins with understanding the bottlenecks that constrain the amount of work that can be done. Alex discovers that the only capacity that matters is the bottleneck capacity. If a new machine is bought in an area that is not a bottleneck, the company is not better off. In fact, instead of improving performance, this type of decision reduces profits because it increases waste: the new machine does not improve the performance of the system as a whole. Instead, it quite likely sits idle, waits for work that is held up somewhere else in the process.

When a plant or office is designed or a new machine is added to the existing structure of the plant or back-office, waste is often the result. Rather than balancing the abilities or capacity of the various machines and people, each machine is bought separately using an isolated analysis of costs and benefits that often don't materialize. Because these decisions are being made one part at a time, rather than in a systemic fashion, the outcome is an unbalanced system that has high levels of built-in idle capacity that are difficult to eliminate.

The Waste That Comes from "Un's"

Waste can be designed into an organization, resulting in excess resources. It can also come from a series of "un's." What is an "un"? It is an unfocused process, undeveloped human capability, unclear mission, unempowered workers, and so on. "Un's" are the result of not adding the "software" needed to maximize the performance of the organization to the physical elements of its systems. "Un's" are lost opportunities and wasted capabilities—all the invisible elements of an organization that make it special.

The impact of the "Un's" on an organization has been a major theme of the total quality management movement. Often described as the "whole person" concept, the objective of TQM is to use both the brains and the brawns provided by a workforce. It's a logical concept, but a review of the level and type of training done by most American corporations suggests that this commonsense idea is not commonly applied. The waste of human potential is a difficult thing to measure, and the improvements in the human capital of the firm that result from good training and development policies are equally nebulous. Yet in a society that is increasingly dominated by service industries whose assets walk out the door every night, the waste of a good mind is the most damaging waste of all.

Unclear missions and unfocused processes also create waste by having good people do less than desirable things (in terms of long-term value maximization). If no one is really clear about the goal, structure, and focus of the organization and its value chains, then it is highly probable that many of the activities completed and results pursued by individuals and groups inside that company will be unnecessary and wasteful. In such a setting, keeping busy is the goal, but busy people do not mean that money is being made. Instead of profit, the entire exercise may be creating waste. It might be better if everyone took a nap. Activity for activity's sake is just another way to throw money out the window: it is "un"necessary.

Complexity: The Insidious Profit Bandit

Idle people, unnecessary activities, and idle machines are one thing, but the waste that is built into an organization because of unnecessary complexity is quite a different problem. Where does complexity come from? It seems to grow unnoticed as a company develops over the years. Complexity, which has both static and dynamic components, is driven by variety: How many parts, how many paths, how many steps, how many people, and how many relationships combine to make up an organization, and how often do all these elements change? It is a case where more means more—more cost, more non-value-added work, more time and money needed to coordinate and control the organization, and more waste.

Complexity is created when work is added to an existing organization without clearly thinking through the path that work will follow through the company or the number of transactions it will create along the way. A simple example of this unnecessary complexity was recently uncovered in a small metal machine shop in Pennsylvania. At this company, subcontracting had slowly become an intricate part of filling almost every customer order. The back-office routines used to handle subcontracting work, though, had been designed early in the company's history, at a time when few subcontractors were used. The accepted procedure was simple: each subcontracted order was placed on its own purchase order, scheduled for shipment to the company doing the work, and controlled through a set of "in-out" cards maintained on the plant floor. To note that a production order was with a subcontractor, the plant clerk simply wrote *SUB* in red on the shop packet and set it aside until the work returned from the subcontractor.

This system seems workable—until you start stirring up the pot a bit to include 250 to 300 possible subcontractors, split orders that result in partial shipments on a regular basis, and the development of a just-in-time supplier relationship with most of the company's major customers. The result? Soaring complexity caused the back office to become the bottleneck for the organization. Fortunately, blanket orders and increasing efforts to simplify the subcontracting business are beginning to cut through the complexity at this company, reducing it once again to a manageable level. But the accumulated waste (lost profits, decreased cash flows, and unhappy customers) resulting from this uncontrolled growth is a reality the company will have to live with for a long time.

The lesson in this example is simple: complexity creeps up on a company as incremental changes in the nature of its business increase the number of transactions and their variety and reduce the amount of time allowed for a response. The dual squeeze of more work in less time (e.g., with fewer resources) creates blow-outs throughout the organization. These problems can turn into witch hunts unless the real sources of the problem—complexity and the waste it creates—are recognized.

USING THE SYSTEM WISELY—OR NOT SO WISELY

Obviously, the highest type of efficiency is that which can utilize existing material to the best advantage.

JAWAHARLAL NEHRU (4)

When a system is designed, boundaries are drawn around the value, as well as the waste, that it can create. How much value versus waste is generated depends on how the organization uses its resources. Three major ways that waste is created in the way that a system is used include "re's," interrupts, and variation in how work is done. No matter which form this waste of resources takes, its effect is the same: profits and future growth are lost.

"Re's" or the "Play It Again, Sam" Approach to Management

If you want to get a quick read on the relative amount of waste a company has, just ask its people to talk about the "re's." What is a "re"? It is anything that is done over again. The most common "re" is rework. It would be hard to find anyone who likes rework, thinks it's a great idea, or believes it increases the profits of the firm. Rework means one thing and one thing only: a mistake has taken place.

To state that a mistake has been made is not to point a finger in the search for someone to blame. That could lead to more "re's"— renegotiation of a labor contract or retraining the workforce. In fact, most mistakes are caused by bad methods, bad materials, and problems with machinery: only a small number are caused by people. And if the problem is people-centered, it is probably rooted in poor training. That is a lesson companies are learning across the globe as the effects of the continuous-improvement model are felt.

One "re" is currently very popular in the trade press and is a "hot" topic in management circles today: "re"engineering. What is reengineering? It is the restructuring of an organization to match its structure to the way work flows through it, and to eliminate waste wherever it is uncovered. Reengineering is top-management driven, unlike the bottom-up approach to eliminating waste common to TQM. Focused on the waste created by a faulty structure, the benefits of reengineering are argued to exceed its cost. As with any form of "re" this is a basic requirement for undertaking the action. If the changes driven by the reengineering efforts create a more flexible, responsive, cost-effective, and quality-focused company, then it is quite likely a good use of resources. As with any form of waste removal, though, keeping an eye on the cost-benefit ratio is a critical part of ensuring that the results of this "re" make the effort worthwhile.

What is interesting about the "re's" is that they seem to multiply, creating more waste as they move along. How so? If we return to the most common "re," rework, we can see the domino effect of this type of waste on the organization. When rework is done, the value added from the first pass at doing the job or finishing the product is thrown away. That's the starting point, or basic cost, of the decision to try to salvage a part or product that has defects.

Reworking the part or product triggers a need for retesting, reinspecting, repackaging, retagging, removing the item, redoing the paperwork, reentering the inventory transactions, and so on. Because the process of creating value is the result of a broad number of interrelated activities and tasks, a mistake that takes place at any one place in the value-creation chain impacts other areas. You can isolate some of this effect by centralizing all the required activities in one rework department, but it will be a department dedicated to waste. Wouldn't it be better to figure out how to prevent the mistake in the first place? That is the only way to eliminate the "re's" from the picture.

Creating Waste by Interrupting the Flow

Interruptions are a part of daily life in most organizations. It seems that as soon as you begin to wade through the pile of papers on the corner of your desk, the telephone rings, a facsimile message comes in, or your "supplier" drops another bunch of work in your "in" basket. To keep on top of your job, you probably feel you need to juggle six things at a time, without dropping a single ball.

Interruptions actually do interfere with the natural juggling act that defines most jobs, activities, or processes. An interruption diverts attention away from the task at hand, places additional stress on the system, and can lead to "fumbles" in the handling of the interrupted work. What are some common interruptions? The telephone is probably the greatest single source of interruption in anyone's life. It seems to ring the most when you least want it to. But in a business this form of interruption is vital to the smooth functioning of the organization and the delivery of quality service to customers.

Other interruptions in organizations are not quite as beneficial. In a factory, the most common interruption is a "hot" order. A "hot" order is one that has to be filled in less than the normal lead time. To meet this tight deadline, the order is routed ahead of other jobs, often interrupting a long run on a machine. This interruption leads to "re's" (they're everywhere)—resetting up the machine and re-routing other work. Unscheduled work is a major cause of waste in a factory or an office.

In reality, even scheduled setup time is an interruption or form of waste. When a machine is down for setup, waste is being generated via lost profits and idle resources. Recognition of the negative effect of setup time on the flow of goods through a company has led many manufacturers to rapidly adopt computer numerical control (CNC) machines and "quick changeover" techniques. The waste caused by the interruption "setup" illustrates the impact of assumptions on the way processes are managed. Changing the machine over is required, but if it is seen as waste rather than value adding, this interruption in the flow of products will be minimized.

Any time the smooth flow of work through a plant or an office is interrupted for inspection, storage, move, setup, or any other activity, it creates idle resources and other forms of waste. The more uncommon the interruption, the more waste it is likely to create as the organization struggles to meet the unexpected demand on its time and resources. If you want to get rid of waste, get rid of unnecessary or excessive interruptions.

The Costs Caused by Variation

The final "flow-based" cause of waste in a company is variation. What is variation? It is unevenness, irregularity, and differences in the way things are done over time. Variation makes it difficult to reap the benefits of the learning curve. Because it represents a shift in the nature of work, variation requires new procedures or, worse yet, can lead to additional work or rework.

Statistical process control (SPC) is a technique being used by many companies to control variation in their manufacturing processes. As shown in Figure 2.3, SPC charts are pictures of the system's desired steady state (the standard) and the amount of deviation away from this standard that can be absorbed by the system (the control limits). SPC charts, maintained by a worker at the point of action, clearly signal when variation has moved beyond acceptable limits. These charts help decrease the total cost of making products by eliminating most of the rework caused by parts that are out of tolerance.

The efficiency of an operation is inversely related to the amount of variation that has to be dealt with. As variation goes up, efficiency goes down—and cost goes up due to increased levels of waste. Henry Ford was one of the first businesspeople to actively address the effect of variation on efficiency through the development of interchangeable parts and the assembly line that resulted from this innovation. The logic used by Ford was simple: handcrafting every automobile made the manufacturing process unduly complex and made downstream servicing of a car difficult. Handcrafted, or unique, parts added an immense amount of variation to the production process. If, instead, parts were made to a prespecified and reliable set of standards, Ford felt that assembly and repair of the automobile could be done better, faster, and cheaper. History has proven Henry Ford to be right. By

FIGURE 2.3 STATISTICAL PROCESS CONTROL

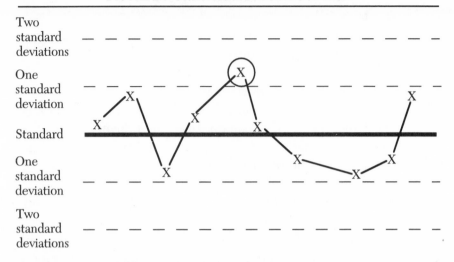

Two standard deviations

One standard deviation

Standard

One standard deviation

Two standard deviations

X = Measurement of output sample's characteristics

o = Deviation that exceeds control boundaries, leading
     to adjustment, stopping of the process

focusing on eliminating waste in every technique he developed, Henry Ford was able to radically change the nature of manufacturing in the Western world.

THE BASICS OF MEASUREMENT

I believe in general in a dualism between facts and the ideas of those facts in human heads.

GEORGE SANTAYANA (1)

Measurements play a key role in the quest to eliminate waste from an organization. To measure something is to make it objective, to place some prescribed value around its characteristics—its defining features. And in so doing, measurements provide a pathway to the mental models needed to transform facts into actions. While many different things can be measured, measurement itself is not a complex task. It is based on a few simple principles and a few basic approaches to using and comparing the characteristics of different events or objects.

We measure things every day. One of the most common ways we do so is by using a standard measurement tool, such as a ruler or a measuring cup, to detail the length or volume of an object before it is used. If a six-inch piece of wood is needed, a ruler will be used to measure this precise length. The key to quality measurement is that the benchmark used to evaluate the object and make decisions to take action based on this information is constant: an inch has to always be an inch, on every ruler, or the concept of length has no meaning.

Basic Measurements

Measurements must be objective and consistent to have any value. They also must be accurate and reliable symbols of the characteristic or event under study. Biased measures, or inconsistent ones, will not provide useful information. With that "golden rule" in hand, what other characteristics define useful measurements? *Basic measurements focus on key characteristics (structure or flow) of an item.* Combinations of these base readings of an object's structure or flow can then be used to create new measures. Some examples of these combinations include:

- Comparison of the measurement for an item over the span of several time periods (focus on *percentage change measures*);

- Comparison of the measurement to a benchmark (*gap measures*);

- Combination of two measures to create a ratio, which is a new measure (*ratio measures*);

- Summation of similar measures to obtain a total (*summary measures*);

- Analysis of the percentage of the "whole" represented by the item measured (*relative percentage measures*).

While all of these measurement options are useful, basic measurement begins with the ratio equation.

Essentials of Ratio Measurement

Ratio measures are the most common type of measurement used to determine how well certain work is being done. It is the basis for productivity, throughput, and all forms of efficiency-based measurements. Ratio measures are so prevalent because they focus on the relationship between two items of importance in the value-creation formula. Whenever two different but related measurements are brought together, the focus turns toward their interrelationship and its impact on the firm's profitability (see Figure 2.4).

Ratio-based measurements are used as the basic measurement tool in this book. When using ratio measurements, it is always important to remember that the ratio will change in value if either the numerator (top number) or denominator (bottom number) is changed. That means we can focus on changing either the top or the bottom number, or their relationship, in order to achieve a targeted performance improvement.

The final message that comes with any discussion of measurements is to remember their power. Measurements lead to behaviors—some good, some undesirable. In fact, measurements can create dysfunctional behavior in organizations if not used wisely. A measurement should be used for information gathering and decision support, but it should never be seen as a form of "truth." While there may be beauty in measurements, their "truthfulness" is less constant. Good measures can be used wisely to target waste and focus improvement efforts. Bad measures can simply create more waste. As each new measure for waste is developed it is important to consider its *behavioral effect*. Different measures, in different settings and in different organiza-

FIGURE 2.4 BUILDING RATIO MEASUREMENTS

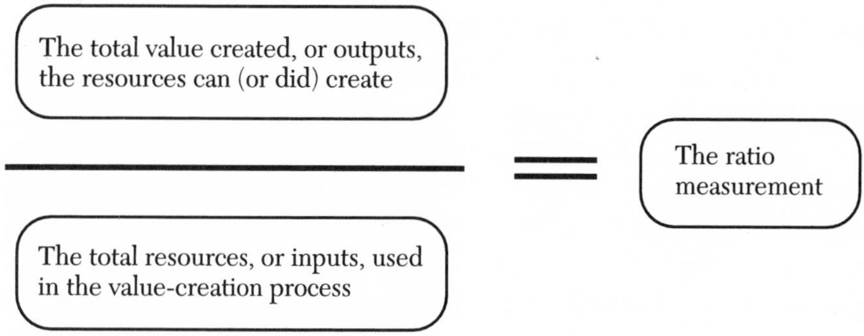

Ratio measurements compare inputs to outputs, either in unit or dollar terms, to focus in on their relationship.

tions, can yield very different results. Every measure a company uses has to be chosen with a careful eye to its existing structure, culture, and strategy.

COST VERSUS WASTE: FINAL COMMENTS

He who buys what he needs not, sells what he needs.

JAPANESE PROVERB (4)

The world of business is a world of scarce resources and ever-growing demands. To grow and prosper in this setting, a company has to use each resource at its command in the best way possible. At the very least, every cost has to yield even greater benefits. If it doesn't, the organization gradually loses its focus. Like a balloon with a slow leak, a company with high levels of waste withers away.

When a company wastes its resources, it is stealing from its own future. Every dollar that is wasted is a dollar that can't be used to generate profits—to create value for the customer. This non-value-added cost, or waste, is a cancer that eats away at the health of the organization, leaving it ultimately unable to sustain itself. And, like a cancer, waste has to be eliminated if an organization is going to prosper and grow.

By now it should be clear that waste is everywhere. Waste is created by the assumptions used to manage an organization or design a product. If setup time is assumed to be a critical, and unchangeable, part of making a product, then this form of waste will never be questioned, much less eliminated. If rework is accepted as a necessary part of doing business and is built into the standards that are used to evaluate a plant, it will always be there. If "hot" orders are seen by the company as a sign of its responsiveness to customer needs, these interruptions and the "re's" they cause will never go away: in fact, they will probably increase in number.

Waste emerges naturally in the evolution of a company. Since growth is a fragmented, incremental event, it gradually draws every-one in the company into habits and procedures that are ineffective in the face of increases in the amount and type of work completed. Procedures that work when business is slow and there is ample time (slack) to deal with problems become unwieldy as the organization becomes more complex.

Waste can be seen and eliminated only if a systemic approach to the company and its processes is taken. If you look at only one part of the organization, you won't be able to see the real impact of a decision to push a "hot" order through a plant. If a company focuses on the cost of the rework department alone—without recognizing that rework creates new work and other forms of "re" work throughout the organization—it will be lulled into thinking that rework is good. It reduces scrap, doesn't it?

Eliminating waste and maximizing profits go hand in hand. Waste, not cost, needs to become the focus of the measurements a company uses to evaluate its progress and ensure its future potential for growth. Waste, not cost, provides a sound basis for improvement. The key to the future is all in a simple word—*waste*.

The most effective way to ensure the value of the future is to confront the present courageously and constructively.

Rollo May
Man's Search for Himself (1)

CHAPTER 3

The Efficiency Mirage

To reach something good it is very useful to have gone astray, and thus acquire experience.

SAINT TERESA OF AVILA (1)

Measurements play a central role in the management of Western organizations. These focused numbers are used to evaluate people, control processes, communicate results against goals, and keep top management in touch with the daily events that shape the organization and its profitability. If a company implements total quality management (TQM) or any related approach, one of the first action items that appears on management's agenda is the need to measure the results this investment has yielded. Is quality up? Are defect rates down? Is throughput improved? Are we turning out more product—better, faster, and cheaper? How do we know? What are we measuring?

The consequences of not having a full set of measurements were recently seen during a visit to a major bicycle manufacturer in the Midwest. The company had recently implemented TQM and just-in-time (JIT) and had found, as many companies do, that its existing set of measurements worked against the changes these new tools were promoting. Since what was being measured was wrong, the company's management made the decision to stop measuring—period.

What was the result of this decision? Since there wasn't a defined shorthand for describing the work being done or the outcome of these efforts—no measurements, in other words—all information had to be exchanged in meetings. While reports might have done the trick, this company was also "antireport." It saw reports as a way to cover tracks and duck responsibility—a CYA tool rather than a communication device. Meetings were the only way that operational results could be discussed in this company.

This intense use of meetings had the following results:

- Managers spent 75 to 80 percent of each day in meetings;

- Missing a meeting meant missing key information about the plant's performance and current goals;

- Managers worked evenings and weekends to make up for lost time;

- No one was really sure whether the changes made to the plant were working because they couldn't be tied to measurements or profitability; and

- Burnout was beginning to take place.

People can work only so many hours and attend only so many meetings before they lose track of their lives, control of their work, and focus on the only objective that matters—meeting or exceeding customer requirements.

Measurements are an alternative to endless meetings and lengthy reports. Like a picture, they can be used in place of a thousand words. But is the picture painted the one that needs to be seen? Is the artist—the measurements expert—using a pointillistic style (lots of detailed measures) or an impressionistic one (a few global measures)? Is the picture a landscape (focused on the process) or a portrait (focused on results)? Much like a painting, a measurement system is a picture of an organization—its efforts, results, and driving concerns. What is the bottom line in the measurements game—the "golden rule" of management?

You get what you measure and reward.

Measurements affect behavior. That is why they need to focus attention on the "right" things.

EFFICIENCY VERSUS EFFECTIVENESS

Time is inelastic; the more inelastic a resource the greater the need to optimize its utilization.

CALDWELL VAN RODEN (6)

Efficiency and effectiveness are two of the key concepts guiding the measurements process in any organization. *Efficiency,* or *doing things right,* is the basis for most of the measurements used to evaluate a company's operations. *Effectiveness,* or *doing the right things,* is, on the other hand, seldom measured directly. Returning to the ratio that defines the measurement process, we can see the shift in focus caused by these two words (see Figure 3.1).

When a company measures its efficiency, it is putting its emphasis on the *denominator,* or bottom half, of the measurements equation. The question this focus creates is a concern for "How many?" How many outcomes, results, or activities are expected to or did occur in the last month or last year? The underlying assumption, of course, is that more is better—more work with the same resources or more output with less than a proportionate increase in the use of resources. This logic underlies the concept of *economies of scale.* It is a concept that suggests that doing more of one thing, more "scale," will allow for more efficient use of a company's resources—and hence, more profits.

That doesn't sound too illogical, does it? If you can do more and

FIGURE 3.1 EFFICIENCY VERSUS EFFECTIVENESS

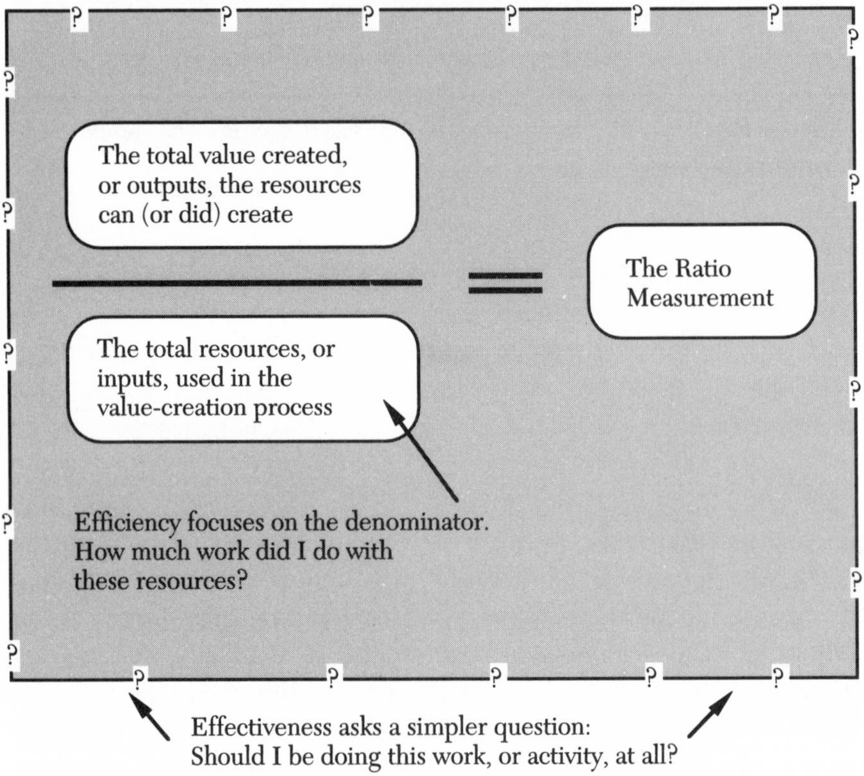

The total value created,
or outputs, the resources
can (or did) create

The total resources, or
inputs, used in the
value-creation process

=

The Ratio
Measurement

Efficiency focuses on the denominator.
How much work did I do with
these resources?

Effectiveness asks a simpler question:
Should I be doing this work, or activity, at all?

more work with the same set of resources, you're doing better, aren't you? Won't increased efficiencies result in a lower cost per unit produced, as fixed costs are spread out over more units? Perhaps, but the only way this logic holds is if everything that is produced or completed by the company is value adding. If any of this activity falls into the pool of waste, potential profits are lost forever. Waste is a form of entropy—leakage—from the system. Once a company's value-creating ability is lost or wasted, it cannot be recovered. Only an infusion of new resources will provide for future growth.

The "Bottoms-up" Approach to Measurement

In focusing on the bottom half, and the bottom half only, of the measurements equation, efficiency measures provide a simple message: do it more, whatever the "it" may be. But when these efficiency measures are applied to one machine or one person or one activity or one output at a time, the overall result can be inefficiency at the systemic or "whole organization" level.

Unfortunately, most measurements used by companies today are efficiency driven. The standard costing system that cranks out product costs and variances from "standard" on a monthly basis is heavily efficiency oriented. Efficiency variances are recorded for labor, materials, and machine utilization. Productivity measures are reported at departmental and global levels—focused on how much work was completed with a set of resources. Throughput measures are used to evaluate how long it took to move a product through the system. Within each of these measurements there is one critical flaw: *whether the work should be done at all is not questioned.* It is assumed that the work being done is needed: the measurements are there only to make sure no one slacks off and that the company gets results for every dollar of its investment in its resources.

The Negative Effects of Efficiency Measures on Performance

The effect of efficiency or "bottom-focused" measurements on JIT and TQM efforts illustrates their weakness. It is common knowledge that over the last few years Wang Computer has not lived up to its promising beginnings. While the causes of this shortfall are many, the measurement system used by the company played a significant role in creating its current problems.

Wang was one of the first companies to implement JIT or cellular manufacturing processes on its plant floor back in the mid-1980s. As with most of the new ideas Wang pursued, JIT and TQM were treated as experiments—trials to be learned from before being fully implemented. The JIT cells at Wang were a tremendous success. Lead times for circuit boards were shaved from a company high in excess of six months to less than one day. Defects were practically eliminated in the cell, and line workers were enthusiastic and supportive of the changes taking place. But the cell was an experiment. That meant that the cell *was not measured* or held accountable to the company's existing measurements and standards. The experiment was left alone: no traditional measurements were applied to it.

This success story might have continued forever, with the cell doing a better job every day at delivering high-quality product to its customer, the Wang assembly area. But when the cell exceeded the performance of the entire plant in terms of productivity (total good units produced per dollar of resources required), management felt it was time to take the JIT cell out of experimental mode and make it the template for changing the entire organization.

When the JIT cell was moved from its experimental status, however, it began to be held accountable for its performance against the company's existing measurements. Efficiency measurements, such as labor efficiencies, were an integral part of the company reporting package. Labor efficiency focuses on the number of direct labor hours used to make a product. A JIT cell, though, changes the work in an area radically. Direct labor is often found performing indirect, or support, work—doing whatever is necessary to maintain a smooth flow of product through the cell.

A JIT cell will perform very poorly against traditional efficiency measures in most cases because of the way it redefines workflows and assignments. At Wang, the cell did not fare well against Wang's labor-efficiency standards. The result? Instead of changing its measurements, management began to put pressure on the cell to improve its performance. Faced with the choice of meeting labor efficiency standards or finding another job, the cell supervisor chose to meet standard. To do so, he slowly allowed batches of work-in-process inventory to creep back onto the plant floor, mucking up the flow of work through the cell. Six months after the JIT cell was returned to the company's traditional reporting system, the cell failed. It was destroyed by labor-efficiency measures applied where they didn't belong. JIT had focused on doing the right things, but the reward system drove people to simply do more—whether what was done was right or wrong.

EFFECTIVENESS: DOING THE RIGHT THING

All effort is in the last analysis sustained by faith that it is worth making.

ORDWAY TREAD
The Art of Leadership (1)

Assumptions lie at the heart of every measurement and every approach to managing organizations. *When a company measures efficiency, it is assuming effectiveness*—that it is using resources to do the right things. Effectiveness seems to be unquestioned and unquestionable by the majority of people who spend their lives within an organization. Or is it? How often have you overheard someone mutter, "This is the dumbest thing anyone has ever asked me to do!" Epitaph delivered, the activity that makes no sense is then done, to the best of the person's ability. Should it have been done at all? No. But then, this question is asked and answered not by the person requesting the work but by the individual doing the job.

One of the major thrusts of the "Japanese" management approach is its focus on the question "Why?" While the blush may have left the rose in terms of the popularity of some of the tools and concepts embedded in the Japanese, or more accurately, *systemic approach* to management, there is little doubt that an intense concern with *what* is being done and *why* it is being done remains a driving force for change in business today. Reengineering, for instance, is a distinctly American tool that asks the "what" and "why" questions using a top-down view of the organization and the value of the activities it performs. "Asking why five times" whenever a problem occurs still remains an essential characteristic of the learning organization.

Effectiveness, then, means that a company knows that the work it is doing, the efforts of its people, are focused on doing the right things—

the activities and outputs a customer values. It is an *"outside in" view of the organization* that sheds new light on old questions and can radically change the strategic direction and operational management of a firm (see Figure 3.2). Effectiveness asks us to focus on what we are doing and why—before we do anything, before any waste is incurred. Effectiveness is based on good planning and on a clear vision or understanding of the value-creation process within an organization. Without effectiveness there is no reason to be efficient. Having good people do the wrong things well is not good management: it is waste.

Shifting Perspectives or Measuring the "Rightness" Factor

Eliminating waste from organizations requires a shift in perspective away from a one-man–one-machine approach to management (efficiency focused) to one based on the precepts of value creation. *Value creation* focuses on *meeting customer requirements.* Emphasizing value creation forces an organization to evaluate the work that it does not in terms of its bottom line or financial performance, but rather in terms of how well it channels its activities into areas that increase customer satisfaction.

How can a company "measure" its effectiveness? Isn't a positive net income number proof that the company is doing what the customer wants? Isn't effectiveness a great idea that can't be put into numbers or made objective? Not really. If you take a systemic view of the organization, effectiveness—or the "rightness" factor—can be designed and implemented successfully.

An example may help clarify how "rightness" can be measured and evaluated. Apple Computer is well known for its innovativeness and the amount of free rein it allows its people to have in setting goals and shaping their work. It is also a company that clearly understands the role of the customer in its future. The entire logic behind an Apple computer system is ease of use as defined by the customer—user-friendliness or meeting the needs of the average customer in a simple, straightforward way.

FIGURE 3.2 EFFECTIVENESS: AN "OUTSIDE IN" VIEW

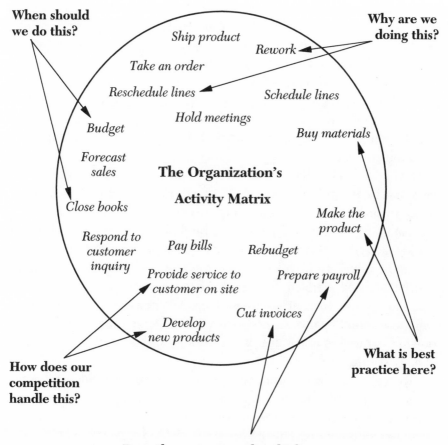

**When should
we do this?**

**Why are we
doing this?**

Ship product

Rework

Take an order

Reschedule lines

Schedule lines

Hold meetings

Budget

Buy materials

Forecast
sales

The Organization's

Activity Matrix

Close books

Make the
product

Respond to
customer
inquiry

Pay bills

Rebudget

Provide service to
customer on site

Prepare payroll

Cut invoices

Develop
new products

**How does our
competition
handle this?**

**What is best
practice here?**

Does the customer value this?

Effectiveness focuses on the "why" behind every activity a
company performs. Measuring effectiveness stops waste before it
is embedded in the activity matrix.

In meeting its customer needs, though, Apple has unconsciously applied many traditional assumptions to how it structures its work and channels employee efforts. This became clear in a one-day session with controllers assigned to the various product lines the company offers. When asked, "What does your customer want?" the entire group responded, with very little hesitation, "Good service and defect-free computers." The next question seemed obvious, then: "What defines good service?" Once again, with little hesitation, these top-level managers responded, "Customers want to pick up the phone and talk to someone about a problem and get a resolution immediately if not sooner"—the customer wanted ongoing operational support from the company.

Having defined what "good service," or organizational effectiveness, meant at Apple, it was a simple matter to develop a benchmark measure of how well the company was delivering this value to its customers (see Figure 3.3). A fairly straightforward exercise—listing the key activities performed under the "customer-service" umbrella currently, as well as the relative percentage of the company's time and effort that were dedicated to each of these activities—provided a snapshot of the current company focus.[1] When these percentages were multiplied by the customer-service budget, a rough approximation of the number and value of the resources dedicated to each type of activity emerged.

The real "Aha!" came from comparing the estimated financial cost of current activities in the customer-service area against the predefined list of activities that the managers felt were critical elements of customer satisfaction. This comparison yielded a *gap measure*—an estimate of the difference between the current state and the optimal use of the company's resources in this area. Two significant gaps were evident almost immediately. First, the resources in customer service were currently focused on the design, writing, printing, and distribution of computer manuals. Yet this area was perceived by the managers to have little or no value to the majority of Apple's customers. If customers were buying an Apple product because it was perceived to be easy to use, they were unlikely to have the

FIGURE 3.3 PUTTING EFFECTIVENESS TO WORK

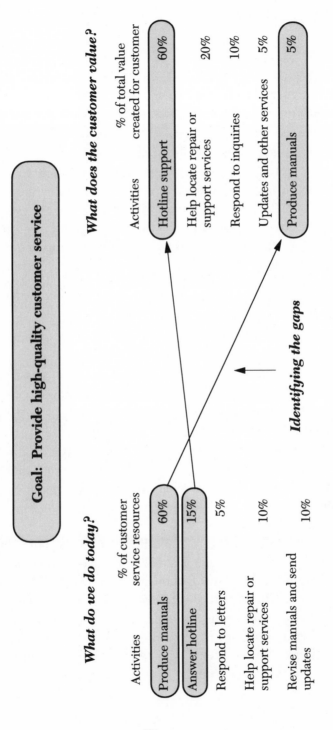

Goal: Provide high-quality customer service

What do we do today?

Activities	% of customer service resources
Produce manuals	60%
Answer hotline	15%
Respond to letters	5%
Help locate repair or support services	10%
Revise manuals and send updates	10%

What does the customer value?

Activities	% of total value created for customer
Hotline support	60%
Help locate repair or support services	20%
Respond to inquiries	10%
Updates and other services	5%
Produce manuals	5%

Identifying the gaps

desire or expertise necessary to read through the detailed manuals that came with the computer. Having the manuals wasn't an error, but their prominence in the overall activity structure of the area was.

The second major gap revealed the same core problem but from its flip side. While the managers felt that a twenty-four-hour hotline was a key element of the service package desired by the company's customers, Apple was spending very little of its resources on this activity. In fact, it appeared that the eighty-twenty rule was at work once again: fewer than 20 percent of the company's resources were dedicated to the activities that generated 80 percent of the customer's satisfaction, or perceived value, with the company's service support. In contrast, almost 80 percent of the resources in this area were focused on activities that yielded less than 20 percent of the total value perceived by customers. Good people were doing a lot of things that weren't contributing to the effectiveness of the entire organization.

Apple Computer is a good company. It is innovative, focused on the value-creation process, and concerned with developing a sustainable competitive advantage by staying close to its customers. Being a good company and *wanting to do the right things,* though, aren't enough. To be better than the competition—and to survive in the intensely competitive global marketplace—Apple has to be sure that it is doing the right things. It has to develop measurements that focus its attention on the only result that really matters: meeting and exceeding customer requirements.

Effectiveness—or the outside-in view of a company or its processes—is simply common sense. Effectiveness measures change the perspective of the organization away from how well it is doing the work it set out to do and toward doing those things, and only those things, that a customer is willing to pay for. By examining the gap between current performance and optimal performance, effectiveness measures direct attention to the value-creation process as defined by the market and not by the company's managers.

Measuring the "Gap" or Waste: The Key to Effectiveness

Developing a sound measure of a company's effectiveness begins with seeing what it is doing right and wrong—from the customer's perspective. This intense focus on the customer—on evaluating the entire system in terms of value creation—sets effectiveness measures apart from the other "E" word (efficiency). Doing things "right" doesn't matter if the work itself isn't important: making a great buggy whip isn't going to help a company succeed, especially if its customers drive automobiles. Effectiveness measures force a company to make an aggressive, honest evaluation of its performance. Nothing is hidden when they are used: waste is revealed in all its unfortunate splendor.

Effectiveness measures examine the difference between what is and what could be. They identify the *expectations gap* between current activities and optimal performance. Effectiveness-driven gap measures provide the impetus needed for a company to continuously improve. They clearly identify what the nebulous term *improve* really means in clear, definable ways that everyone can understand. Gap measures driven by the customer also remove much of the politics from the change process. It is hard to argue that the company's success is *not* based on meeting customer needs.

Effectiveness measures, then, draw attention to the waste that is taking place in the organization every day, whether that company does things the "right" way or not. They help an organization identify its strengths and weaknesses and facilitate the changes needed to improve a company's competitive position. Superior even to benchmarking data, effectiveness measures hold a company to a stringent standard: customer expectations. These measures don't simply ask whether a company is performing its work as well as, or better, than another company. They ask whether any of the work being done, in any setting, is really what should be done. Measuring any other aspect of a company's performance, without first developing sound effectiveness measures, is like putting the cart before the horse: the company simply won't get where it's going. Are effectiveness measures confined to the global or "whole company" level? Not really. In fact, the best way to tackle the waste caused by "re's" is by focusing on effectiveness.

"RE'S" AND OTHER NOT-SO-RIGHT ACTIVITIES

Results! Why, man, I have gotten a lot of results. I know several thousand things that won't work.

THOMAS A. EDISON (4)

High-level discussions and conceptual tools aren't necessary to convince anyone that a "re" isn't the best way to use a company's scarce resources. A "re" means that a mistake has been made, that something has to be done a second time (or a third or a fourth), but the value this activity creates occurs only once. No matter how many times Thomas Edison found out what didn't work, the only experiment he conducted that created value was the one that finally resulted in the development of the light bulb. Was knowledge gained from all of the mistakes? Undoubtedly Edison felt this to be the case. But few people were willing to pay Edison for his mistakes, no matter how much he learned in the process of making them.

"Re's" aren't the only activities a company performs on an ongoing basis that run counter to the concept of effectiveness. Many activities shouldn't be done at all, even if the overall output of the process they are part of does create value for the customer. Activities that serve as interruptions to the workflow, that create or are necessary to respond to variation, and that are the outgrowth of unduly complex procedures all result in wasted resources and reduced profitability.

Measuring the Waste in the "Re's"

Effectiveness measures are focused on the gap between what is and what should be. Measuring the "re's" from an effectiveness perspective, then, starts with identifying the amount of resources that are

FIGURE 3.4 MEASURING THE WASTE IN A "RE"

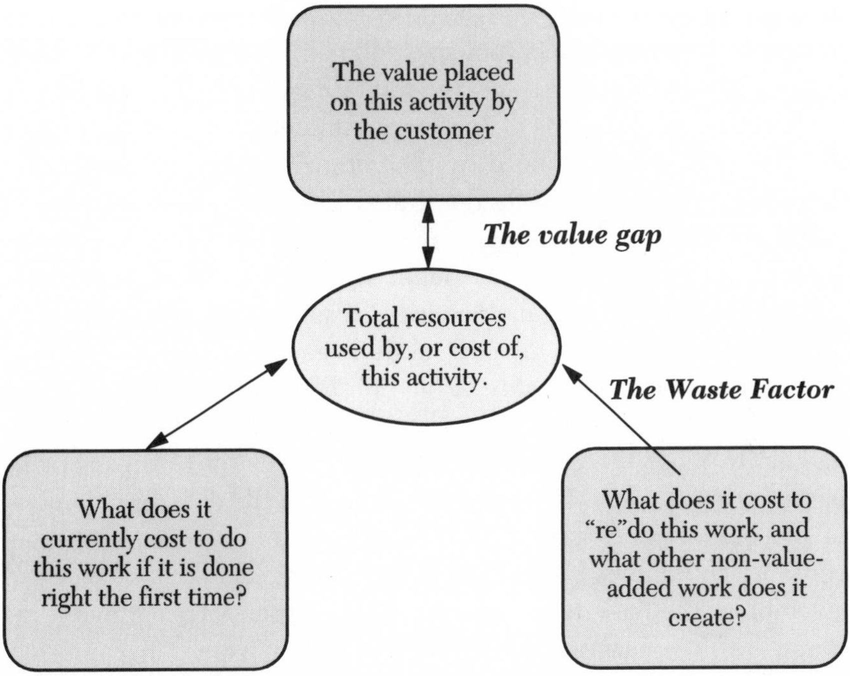

The value placed
on this activity by
the customer

The value gap

Total resources
used by, or cost of,
this activity.

The Waste Factor

What does it
currently cost to do
this work if it is done
right the first time?

What does it cost to
"re"do this work, and
what other non-value-
added work does it
create?

used up by an activity or sequence of activities when it is done right
the first time (see Figure 3.4).

It might seem better to start with evaluating the amount of value
created by the activity, in general, against customer expectations, but
if we did so, it would be hard to separate the cost of the "re's" from the
waste generated by unnecessary activities in general. Since the "re's"
are one of the easiest forms of waste to measure and eliminate, as well
as the most bothersome form of waste we encounter in organizations,
it is best to keep them clearly in sight during the measurement
process.

The key element in developing a measurement of the waste generated by a "re" is to identify how it ripples across the organization
leaving waste in its path. The full cost of any "re" has to include all the

related activities it triggers or makes necessary. The waste created by a mistake is all the avoidable cost it pulls with it. An *avoidable cost* is one that would go away if the mistake weren't made—a cost that is the direct outcome of a "re."

An example from a medium-size company that produces holiday candies and baskets illustrates the total impact of the "re's." Facing intense pressure from one of its major customers to reduce the cost of the Easter baskets produced by the company, Eastern Candy[2] decided to find a new source for the stuffed Easter bunnies that serve as a central feature of the baskets. Early in January, a new source for the Easter bunnies was found. The supplier guaranteed that it could get all the bunnies the company needed at a substantial price reduction ($1.05 per bunny versus the current $1.35 each).

After reviewing the quality of the bunny with the customer, Eastern's management decided to order the 250,000 Easter bunnies it needed to meet the customer order. Production of the rest of the basket's goodies went forward on schedule. As the date for shipment of the baskets drew nearer, Eastern's president began to be concerned. The bunnies hadn't been delivered yet, and the lead time for assembling the baskets was getting short. Expediting, one often ignored "re" (*re*contacting the supplier, and *re*verifying, ship dates) led to endless *re*scheduling of the assembly team. The troubles for this company were just beginning, though.

With little time to go before Eastern would be in default on its order to its major customers, the expediting heated up. In desperation, the purchasing manager contacted the source of the bunnies—an Asian manufacturer—directly. The bunnies weren't even in production yet. The scheduled ship date from the factory was May 15—after Easter!

No bunnies meant no baskets and no business. As the company struggled to respond to this emergency, the waste began to mount. The company had to *re*contact the customer to explain the situation, *re*negotiate the type and number of stuffed animals required, *re*identify viable suppliers (who now had to have the stock in hand), *re*negotiate the contract prices (with little or no ability to reject exorbitant pricing or lesser quality goods), *re*schedule the plant once again, and *re*enter all necessary transactions. Overtime, an "excess," was the only solution left to the company. And once the baskets were completed, air freight had to be used to get them to the customer's stores on time.

Of course, in the rush to get the stuffed animals in and to complete the order, errors were made. *Re*work soared, as workers tried desperately to get the baskets put together faster. The rework resulted in the hiring of temporary workers to fix the errors. The baskets got out, but the "savings" the company had hoped for turned into major losses. One mistake—not questioning the reliability of the supplier before giving all of the business to it—led to a cascading growth of errors and expense.

The story doesn't end there, of course. The original 250,000 bunnies did arrive in late May. 250,000 bunnies take up a lot of space. Now the company is faced with *re*locating the bunnies, *re*inspecting them every time they are used to ensure they haven't been damaged in the interim, and *re*financing them each and every period they remain in the plant. It's an Easter story without a happy ending and a poignant example of the escalating nature of waste.

Hidden Activities That Cause Waste

The second part of the analysis of the effectiveness of any process is to clearly identify whether the activities being performed the *right way* really need to be done at all. The major challenge in this approach is pinpointing the optimal set of activities required to deliver value to the customer. A second challenge lies in identifying all the work that is really taking place. The first challenge requires the company to use some form of external evaluation of its processes, such as benchmarking. The second challenge brings a company face to face with all the invisible forms of waste hidden in its assumptions and structure.

Evaluating the "best" way to do work is difficult. Making this evaluation in an objective, productive manner is even more so. Many avenues are open for gaining this information or perspective. Within a company, a brainstorming team, left unfettered by politics and other considerations, can often identify the core list of essential activities. In other cases, outside information can provide the necessary impetus for change. Hiring a consultant to evaluate your current processes is a second way to incorporate the *effectiveness perspective* into an organization. Finally, some form of benchmarking—whether internal, competitive, industry, or best-in-class—can be used to better understand activities that seem to be a necessary part of meeting customer requirements.

The outcome of this exercise to gain the effectiveness perspective is a "straw-man" model of a process (see Figure 3.5) that allows a company to meet or exceed customer requirements without the use of excessive resources or activities (minimal waste). If internal benchmarking is the basis for developing the straw man, it is important to ensure that every unit that is being compared against the "best" feels it is good at some element of the model set of activities. Ownership of an internally developed straw-man model is critical to its success in helping focus the change efforts of the organization.

With a sound straw-man model in place, gap measures between current activities being performed to do work and an optimal approach to doing this work can be developed. The first gap measure would be a simple list of current activities and their emphasis versus the list of ideal activities and their emphasis. The second gap measure would focus on the total dollars spent on resources in this area, as well as the amount of resources expended on specific elements of this process, as compared to the best-case scenario or straw-man model. These two gap measures provide a sound reading on the effectiveness of current operations and the amount of absolute change that needs to take place.

Avon Products used this type of effectiveness measurement approach to improve its service to various sales agents scattered across the globe. A straw-man model of best practice among all the company's regional sales offices provided a clear picture of what was being done right, what was being done "wrong," and how to refocus the efforts of the regional supervisors on activities and outcomes that were valued by the customer. Resources were shifted using the results of

FIGURE 3.5 "STRAW MAN" MODELS AND EFFECTIVENESS

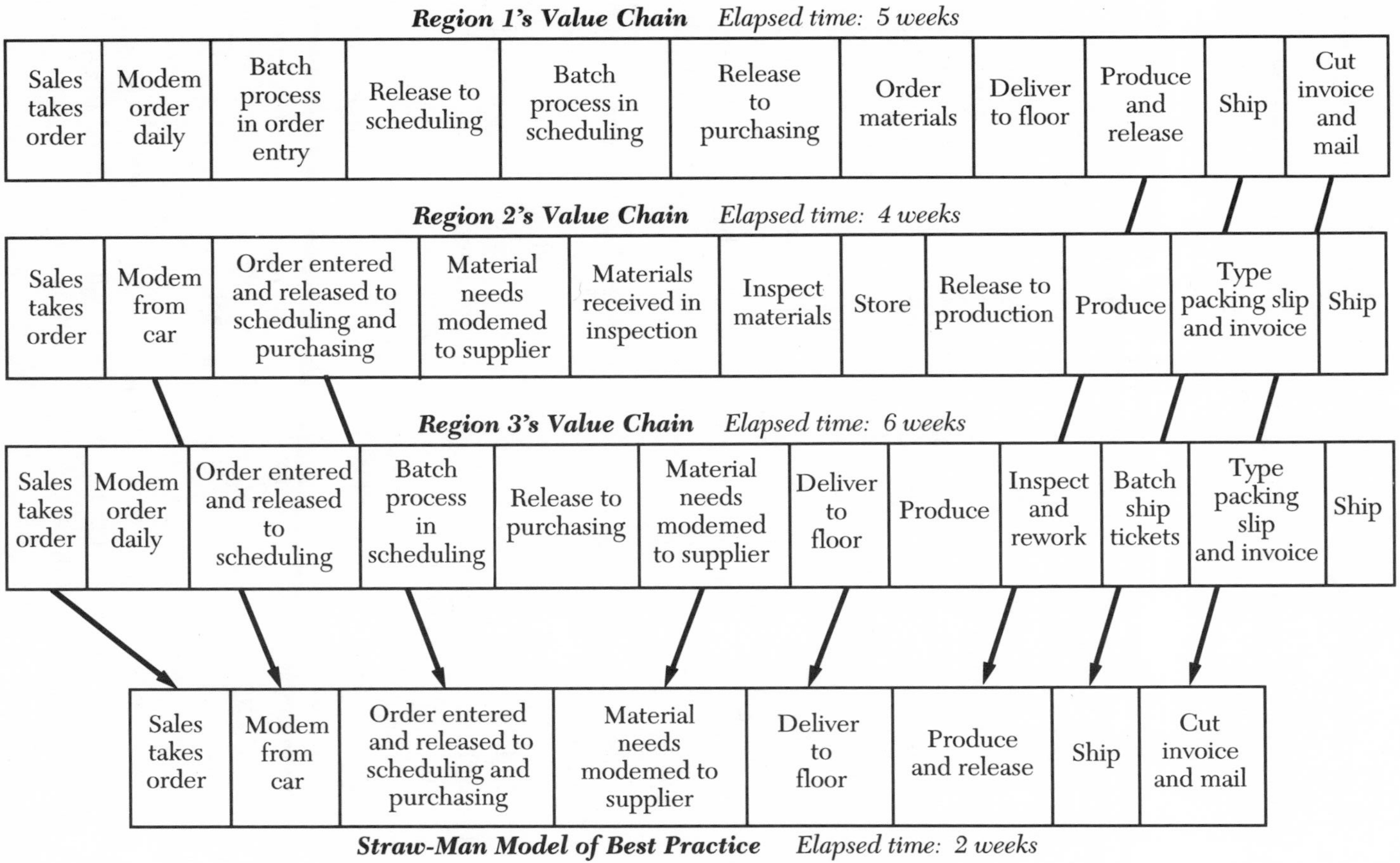

Region 1's Value Chain *Elapsed time: 5 weeks*

Sales takes order	Modem order daily	Batch process in order entry	Release to scheduling	Batch process in scheduling	Release to purchasing	Order materials	Deliver to floor	Produce and release	Ship	Cut invoice and mail

Region 2's Value Chain *Elapsed time: 4 weeks*

Sales takes order	Modem from car	Order entered and released to scheduling and purchasing	Material needs modemed to supplier	Materials received in inspection	Inspect materials	Store	Release to production	Produce	Type packing slip and invoice	Ship

Region 3's Value Chain *Elapsed time: 6 weeks*

Sales takes order	Modem order daily	Order entered and released to scheduling	Batch process in scheduling	Release to purchasing	Material needs modemed to supplier	Deliver to floor	Produce	Inspect and rework	Batch ship tickets	Type packing slip and invoice	Ship

Straw-Man Model of Best Practice *Elapsed time: 2 weeks*

Sales takes order	Modem from car	Order entered and released to scheduling and purchasing	Material needs modemed to supplier	Deliver to floor	Produce and release	Ship	Cut invoice and mail

59

Avon's internal benchmarking study, allowing the company to deliver consistently high-quality service across its entire distribution network.[3]

Measuring the Waste of Invisible Activities

One of the most valuable tools that companies have begun to use to study their workflows is process analysis. Process-analysis tools are used to develop detailed maps of the work performed by a company to meet a specific customer request for service. Drawing up these maps, which are usually the result of a team collaborative effort, is a lesson in itself for the company. Seldom has anyone in the company actually traced the path an order follows through the plant and back office. The results of this tracing are often distressing. At one small company, management found that it was promising two-week delivery on items that took over four weeks to pass through the back office. No wonder the plant was always in a crisis: by the time it received the order, it was already two weeks late!

Good process maps list all ongoing activities, whether or not they are invisible. Process, move, planned delays, unplanned delays, inspections, setups, sorting, batching, and all other tasks performed are laid out in detail. This information is usually accompanied by an estimate of the amount of time it takes to complete each activity and the total number of output units that are yielded by this effort.

The most common outcome of process mapping is a group question: "Why do we do that?" When a workflow is diagrammed in detail, it is usually obvious that improvements can and should be made. As the number of delays, moves, setups, inspections, sorting, batching, and other non-value-added activities are tallied, the magnitude of the changes needed becomes evident (see Table 3.1). If the resource cost of performing these activities is added to the analysis, the prime candidates for improvement efforts are easy to spot. What is being eliminated by these efforts? The waste that comes from the *invisible activities*—the nonprocess work—that is often overlooked in the push for increased productivity and throughput.

TABLE 3.1 MEASURING EFFECTIVENESS GAPS

> Time wasted translates to lost profit potential. → Effectiveness gaps

Region 3's value chain		Best-practice value chain		Effectiveness gaps
Sales takes order	1 hour	Sales takes order	1 hour	None
Modem orders daily	1 day	Modem from car	5 min.	1 day
Order entered and released to scheduling	1 hour	Order entered and released to scheduling and purchasing	1 hour	None
Batch process in scheduling	1 day			1 day
Release to purchasing	1 day			1 day
Material needs modemed to suppliers	1 hour	Material needs modemed to suppliers	1 hour	None
Deliver to floor	3 weeks	Deliver materials to floor	1 week	2 weeks
Produce	2 days	Produce and release	2 days	None
Inspect and rework	1 week			1 week
Batch ship tickets	1 day			1 day
Type packing slip and invoice	1 day			1 day
Ship	3 days	Ship	3 days	None
		Cut invoice and mail	10 mins.	None
	6 weeks		2 weeks 3 hours	4 weeks

The higher the number, amount of time required by, or cost of these invisible activities, the less effective the process is at delivering value at minimal cost to its customers. Effectiveness measurements can be made across each of these dimensions, once a straw-man model of "no waste" is developed. The performance gaps identified by this exercise pinpoint the areas where attention should be focused to gain the maximum improvement, in terms of total process effectiveness. The goal is simple: make sure the company is doing the right thing.

AN INTOLERANCE FOR WASTE

As the gardener, by severe pruning, forces the sap of the tree into one or two vigorous limbs, so should you stop off your miscellaneous activity and concentrate your force on one or a few points.

RALPH WALDO EMERSON (6)

Improving the profitability of a company starts with eliminating waste from its daily activities. Focusing on waste provides the company with a clear focus and target for its improvement efforts. One of the most troubling types of waste in an organization is that due to ineffectiveness—the failure to do only the right things. A customer has clear expectations about the type and amount of value he or she is buying from a company. This defined value is the basis for the price that is offered for the good or service. A customer's price does not build in acceptable levels of waste: it is defined according to value with a bit of profit thrown in to make sure the company can continue to fill these needs.

Eliminating waste from an organization begins with taking an outside-in view of its activities, identifying the optimal mix of activities and resources (a straw-man model), and then focusing everyone's attention on improvements that will bring the company closer to this model of effective performance. An effectiveness perspective is far more valuable than a concern with efficiency. The gap measurements that are the outcome of a focus on effectiveness ensure that improvements efforts yield the optimal benefits for the company and its customers.

Effectiveness is a simple way to describe a complete intolerance for waste. It is the basis for every other type of measurement that is developed in the chapters that follow. When using this tool or any of the ones that are described subsequently, it is critical to ask, "Are we doing the right things? Would our customers willingly pay for these activities? How much do they value them? Do we spend our resources wisely, given what the customer really wants from us in terms of goods and services?" If these questions aren't asked and answered, any others will be pointless. Doing the wrong things better, faster, and cheaper is not a recipe for success but rather the first step on the road to difficult times. Picking the right *E* word—*effectiveness,* not *efficiency*—can highlight a path forward that results in a sustainable competitive advantage built on customer satisfaction—the ultimate goal of any organization.

Life affords no higher pleasure than that of surmounting difficulties, passing from one step of success to another, forming new wishes and seeing them gratified.

SAMUEL JOHNSON (4)

CHAPTER 4

Getting It Right – the First Time

Experience is the name everyone gives to their mistakes.

OSCAR WILDE
Lady Windermere's Fan (7)

There is a basic beauty in the concept of doing a job right the first time—and every time. It is a beauty born of simplicity, an elegance driven by the presence of just the right actions at just the right time by just the right people for just the right reasons. There is no room for the ugliness of waste in this setting: waste mars the vision and destroys the beauty that could have been possible.

Business and art are seldom put together in the same sentence, though. If these two words do appear in the same sentence, it is often in the form of an oxymoron—an illogical stringing together of two concepts. Yet the definition of art suggests that this gap may be more illusory than real:[1]

art (noun)   *The use or employment of things to answer some special purpose; the employment of means to accomplish some end.*

65

If most people were asked to define the term *business,* would not many of the same words be used? In fact, business is normally defined as the employment of means to accomplish a specific end: making a profit. It would seem, then, that the criteria used to judge a work of art—its simplicity, its elegance, the artist's creative use of available materials, the artist's ability to create a vision or image that is greater than the sum of its parts, and the linking of form and function to achieve this outcome—are all critical elements of a well-run business.

In the business world, effectiveness (doing the right things or elegance) and efficiency (doing things right or simplicity) are crucial elements of the businessperson's "pallet" of paints and colors. These raw materials are used to create a product or service. The more creative or value creating these products are, the more successful the firm will be *(ceteris paribus)*. The essence of success in business lies in envisioning where the company wants to go, and then integrating and focusing available resources to reach this goal. The paints used by the business "artist" must be applied with a purpose in mind if the final picture is to have a value of its own.

At the heart of planning in a business setting lies the issue of product design and product development. The results of these activities provide the lifeblood of the organization—its future cash streams. A company that is a successful innovator—creating new products from existing materials or creating new materials on a regular basis—will outperform the competition in the long run.

Post-It™ notes are a prime example of 3M's ability to turn failed experiments into successful business ventures. The adhesive used in Post-It™ notes failed to be sticky enough for its original application. But the scientist who developed the adhesive found that when applied to paper, the resulting note could be attached and reattached to various surfaces without losing its stickiness or leaving a mark. This discovery led to one of the most commercially successful ventures 3M has ever had. A new business unit was set up to bring the product to market, and the rest is history.

THE CHALLENGE POSED BY
NEW PRODUCTS AND PROCESSES

All change is not growth; all movement is not forward.

ELLEN GLASGOW (4)

In the mid-1980s, Computer-Aided Manufacturing, International (CAM-I) published a conceptual framework for the development of cost-management systems (CMS).[2] A CMS was an extension of the traditional accounting system used by companies throughout the world. It focused on the effect of product life cycle and development costs on the long-term profitability of the firm and suggested various ways a company could better understand and manage this essential value-creating process.

One core concept put forward by the CAM-I conceptual framework was that most of the costs of making a product are set at the point of design. As described by the authors: "The product specifications usually lock in the majority of materials cost, because the performance characteristics and product costs goals are normally specified. Also, the range of manufacturing processes primarily depends on the materials selected. Thus, design and process decisions can have a long-term impact on a company's cost structure." These arguments were then portrayed in graphical form (see Figure 4.1), resulting in the now well-known life-cycle cost pattern. The logic behind this approach was simple: up to 90 percent of the total cost for making a product was locked in at the point of design. A poor design, it would seem, could destroy all hopes of profitability downstream.

When Enthusiasm Leads the Way

Machine Works, a small company in Pennsylvania, learned the hard way about the importance of design in controlling cost and waste. The entrepreneur owner of the company decided that the company should begin manufacturing its own above-ground lifts, which are used to

FIGURE 4.1 COSTING OUT THE PRODUCT LIFE CYCLE

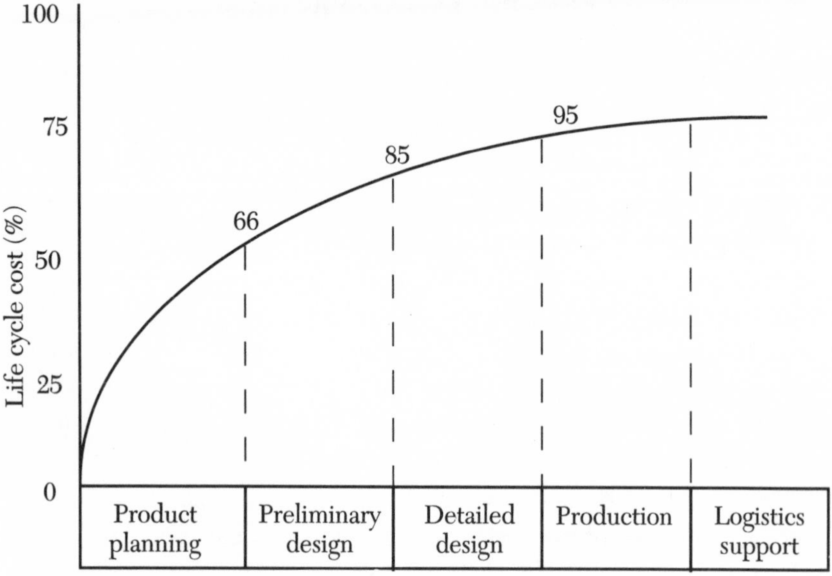

NOTE: This CAM-I figure was adapted from B. S. Blanchard, *Design and Manage to Life Cycle Cost* (Portland, OR: M/A Press, 1978).

raise and lower cars in repair shops. The company had been purchasing these lifts from an outside supplier and then reselling them to a broad range of customers. The motivation for designing and developing a company-built lift was sensible: environmental protection laws were making it harder for garages to obtain permission to install in-ground lifts, the company's core offering in the marketplace. Management felt that above-ground lifts were soon to become the only product viable in the marketplace.

The reasons for designing and developing a company-built lift went beyond Machine Works' concern with market shifts. A second driving issue was the consistently poor quality and performance of the outsourced lifts. It was doubtful the company could build a strong share in this developing market with an inferior product. So the decision was made to design and develop a new above-ground lift that would be sole-sourced by this company.

Entrepeneurial firms, though, have a way of jumping in and simply "doing" rather than planning the design process. In its defense, this was Machine Works' first major product launch. It didn't have history as a guide, only enthusiasm. In addition, to counter the market perception that an above-ground lift with its name on it would be of inferior quality, the decision was made to design a "cadillac" model: it would have more quality and functionality than any competing lifts. It was a solid plan for creating a niche in the market, but there was a slight flaw in the follow-through.

What was this flaw? The design stage was undertaken with a sole focus on the bells and whistles aspect of the lift. Manufacturability, cost versus value, durability, and other key elements of designing a commercially successful product were all but ignored. As a result, the company launched a product at market price that was better in every way than competitive models. The demand for the product was instantaneous. Unfortunately, the lift, as designed, cost $1,000 more to build than the going market price for above-ground lifts. Every time Machine Works shipped one of its new lifts, it was losing $1,000 in hard currency.

Given that 90 percent of the cost is locked in at design, it is easy to see that this company will have a difficult time turning this situation around. On-site value-analysis teams meet almost daily to try to find ways to shave dollars from the cost of the lift. With a high material content as the driving factor focusing these redesign efforts, material after material is being changed as rapidly as engineering can redraw the affected part of the lift, respecify the materials needs, relist the new manufacturing and handling procedures, and so on. In fact, the number of engineering change notices that have been generated by this product exceed the total number caused by the other 10,000 machined parts the company has made over its lifetime.

The moral of the story? Doing things right the first time is the only way to avoid the vast stream of "re's" that a poor design triggers. Every "re" being done in this firm is waste. And given the design problems the company is facing, much of the work that is considered value adding is waste: the company is using up far more resources than the product itself warrants in the eye of the customer. Excess functionality, or the cadillac approach to product design, is as wasteful as the subsequent redesign and rework that fall on the heels of a poorly designed product. Doing too much or too little has the same effect in this setting: waste is built into the product and process, waste that is much harder to eliminate than to create. Only by understanding, measuring, and eliminating the waste embedded in the design process can a company ensure that its efforts will help it achieve its ultimate goal: sustainable growth and profitability.

Issues Surrounding the Design Process

To achieve the goal of "getting it right the first time," companies are addressing a broad range of issues in the product-design process. The first of these was illustrated in the Machine Works example above: functionality versus value. A customer is, for the most part, buying a specific functionality or ability to do work when a product is purchased. Functionality often dominates form in the customer's mind: beauty or art is seldom the primary criterion driving the purchase decision. Machine Works designed a beautiful lift, but the lift was sold to mechanics in garages who knew that the attractive decals and paint job would soon be a faded memory. In the rough and tumble world of automobile repair, the only question everyone wants answered is, "Will it work?" Art is not cast aside; it is defined by the movement or elegance of purpose the product achieves—not its external image. A company that forgets this fact is building waste into the heart of the products and processes it relies upon to survive.

A second major issue in the design process is whether once a product is designed it can be built. Strange as it may sound, many products have been designed that are impossible to manufacture in large numbers. One of the most striking examples of a breakdown between design and manufacturability was seen at a company in the Midwest that makes counters—the devices that keep a running count of the number of parts, copies made, or related events in the production process. These counters were designed to snap together. Once the plastic case was put together, it could not be taken apart again. So doing this assembly activity right the first time was an essential part of learning to make these counters.

Unfortunately, sometimes the design of the counters failed to take into account the human factor. How so? One specific specialty counter was designed in such a way that the assembler had to push in wires all around the edges of the box, keep them internal to the case, and then snap the box shut around all the wires. If any of the wires were visible outside the box, the unit had to be scrapped. The only person in the plant who could successfully make this unit had an extra finger on each hand! The designers had developed a product that no normal human could make. The only days this product could be made were the days this special employee came in. The results of a poor design were high levels of scrap, ineffective use of existing resources, and the creation of a major bottleneck in the production of this unit. Waste was created in terms of inefficiency and scrap because no one had thought about putting the box together.

"Doing the right things" in the design process, then, starts with understanding the customers' real requirements (the value they'll pay for) and the basic manufacturability of the designed unit. But the issues that need to be addressed extend beyond this to include the environmental impact of the materials used and manufacturing process employed, the fit of the proposed product to the company's existing physical and human capacity to do the work, the number and cost of any new machines, processes, or technologies required to successfully produce the item, and finally, the total profit that product will provide over its life cycle. A good design is not one that looks good or has lots of shiny lights and buzzers, but rather one that does what is required, and only what is required, to meet customer needs.

When these simple facts are forgotten, the waste meter begins to tick. Each misstep at the design process drops dollars into the pool of waste, a constant drip, drip, drip of lost profitability, lost potential, and lost opportunities. A poorly executed design can actually open up a huge gash in the side of the organization. Management may try to put a tourniquet on the wound to stop the bleeding (discontinue production), attempt surgery to remove the waste (cost-reduction drives), or treat the worst symptoms of the disease (engineering change notices), but the result is the same. Waste proliferates. The future profit potential of the company is transformed into waste—a loss of value-creating potential that cannot be recovered. Much like an oil spill, the only option left to management after the disaster has occurred is to contain the spill and prevent the amount of damage it does to the company and society.

PREVENTING WASTE: UNDERSTANDING THE GAME BEFORE IT BEGINS

Victorious warriors win first and then go to war, while defeated warriors go to war first and then seek to win.

SUN-TZU (7)

The key to effectiveness in design and development is planning— taking time to ensure that all the pieces of the complex puzzle that make up the development process fit together smoothly with no gaps and no holes. The downside risk remains as a constant reminder of the waste that will be generated if a mistake is made, but what tools or concepts can help prevent the waste before it is too late? What does it take to make seamless development a reality?

Out of all of the new "tools" or approaches that have been developed by business experts over the past fifteen years, *target costing* is the most powerful and promising addition to the corporate tool kit in this area:

Target cost   *A market-based cost that is calculated using the sales price necessary to secure a desired market share as its basis. Market price less desired profit sets the boundary on the total costs. This boundary is the* target cost.

In the opening chapter, the logic of a target cost was used to illustrate the role waste plays in the erosion of a company's profitability. Target costing, then, is an "outside-in top-down" form of accounting that is an intricate part of an effective product-design effort.[3]

Target costing is a cost-control tool that focuses management's efforts on identifying the best product design—the design that meets customer expectations while ensuring an acceptable level of profitability for the firm. Target costing builds from a very basic idea: *when a product is launched, it must earn a profit immediately.* This goal is brought to life through a conscious examination of every resource, every process, and every activity that will be required to build the product or provide the service. The target cost is, quite simply, the most the company can afford to spend on all of its efforts related to the product; if spending exceeds this limit, profits are sacrificed and waste is created.

One of the most straightforward ways to evaluate the effectiveness or degree of waste embedded in the design process is to identify the product's target cost and match current cost estimates against this benchmark. The outcome of this comparison is a gap measure—a solid indication of the amount of cost that has to be taken out of the product *before* it is placed into production (see Table 4.1). Redesigning a product on a computer is much less wasteful than redesigning it on the shop floor as it is being made. But what do you do with this gap measure after you have developed it?

This question brings a company face to face with the cultural biases and the incessant drive to get things done that defines business in the Western world. First, the gap between the target cost and current estimated cost of the proposed design is often quite large. In the Machine Works example, material costs alone were in excess of the company's target cost for the entire production, shipping, distribution, and back-office activities. The gap between desired cost (the target) and actual cost was so large that little of the original product design and structure remains today; the original work lies in piles on the floor, scrap materials, endless engineering change notices, and

TABLE 4.1 GAP MEASUREMENTS FOR CONTROLLING DESIGNED-IN COSTS

Activity/cost item	Estimated cost	Target cost	The "gaps"
Materials: Lift frame	$ 400.00	$ 200.00	
Materials: Lift hydraulics	400.00	150.00	**Materials Gap**
Materials: Arms and assemblies	200.00	150.00	**$500.00**
Total materials	$1,000.00	$ 500.00	
Labor: Weldments	$ 250.00	$ 100.00	
Labor: Assembly	300.00	100.00	**Labor Gap**
Labor: Other	100.00	50.00	**$400.00**
Total labor	$ 650.00	$ 250.00	
Miscellaneous suppport	$ 100.00	$ 50.00	
Overhead	250.00	200.00	**Overhead Gap**
Total overhead	$ 350.00	$ 250.00	**$100.00**

countless blueprint revisions. Waste continues to grow as the company struggles to respond to the realities of the marketplace.

How could a target-costing approach help Machine Works? A target cost should serve as a stoplight: it should prevent problems such as those experienced by Machine Works from happening at all. If the estimated cost is greater than the target cost, the new product or process should not be released. The gap between desired cost and actual cost is harder to close on the production line than on the drawing board. But holding up a new product because of a gap measure—excess cost—requires organizational discipline. Discipline is a commodity that can be hard to come by in a company. In a world of personal incentives, salespeople pushing for new products to gain sales, top management pushing for new sources of profits, and customers wanting better products, faster and cheaper, patience is seldom seen as a virtue.

Yet this patience is a key element of long-term, sustainable growth. New products that are not profitable in the long run are not good investments for the firm. Rather than creating value, they diminish it, as the accumulation of waste caused by these premature launches nibbles away at the profits generated by other products and services. As the old adage goes, "Discretion is the better part of valour." Being willing and able to wait until a product is designed and buildable at or below the target cost is not an option: it is a critical element of corporate survival.

Target Costing: A Life-Cycle Perspective

Changes taking place at Toyota underscore how target costing can be used as a disciplining device. At Toyota, products used to be launched if they were "close" to the target cost. The excess cost was known, and cost-reduction targets were established at the launch date: continuous improvement was relied on to close the gap between actual cost and target cost.

Toyota found out that it was difficult to close this gap, no matter how industriously people on the line created better, faster, and cheaper ways of making the product. In addition, the downward pressure on price, a natural part of the product life-cycle curve (see Figure 4.2), meant that the cost-reduction efforts had to be doubled. In what way? The cost-reduction programs had to yield enough savings to eliminate the gap between the actual cost and target cost *at the launch point as well as absorb the effect of the downward pressure on market price* (which after profit was removed created a new and even lower target cost).

If a company launches a product before its target-cost goals are met, it places itself in a difficult position: it has to double its rate of improvement. In other words, the company *has to beat the learning curve.* It's not good enough to control costs or to slowly reduce them in response to market pressures; a company that launches a product "before its time" has to recoup up-front losses (eliminate waste) as well as move rapidly down the learning curve in terms of overall productive capability.

For Toyota and other companies that conduct business across the globe today, this cost challenge is nearly overwhelming. Waste that has not even occurred must be identified and removed if the company is to recoup its development costs, make a profit on ongoing sales, and ensure ample capital to support future new product and process innovations. What are some of the drivers that can focus this search for better ways to bring new products to market? Several factors appear to be central to the process of successful innovation:[4]

- *Product functionality*   Does the product meet customer expectations in terms of quality, price, delivery, and basic purpose? Is the product more complex than necessary? Does it provide excess capabilities, options, or features? Will it work given the tasks the customer needs performed? Will it work consistently?

- *Product flexibility*   Can the product or process be easily adapted to meet new needs? Can new materials or processes be easily developed or integrated into the product's value chain as new technologies and innovations appear? Can the product be

FIGURE 4.2 THE PRODUCT PROFIT "SQUEEZE"

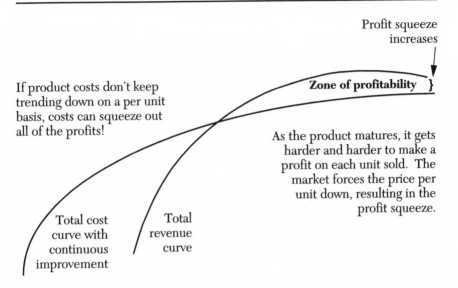

Profit squeeze increases

Zone of profitability }

If product costs don't keep trending down on a per unit basis, costs can squeeze out all of the profits!

As the product matures, it gets harder and harder to make a profit on each unit sold. The market forces the price per unit down, resulting in the profit squeeze.

Total cost curve with continuous improvement

Total revenue curve

"customized" in the customer's eyes with little cost? Has variety been pushed to the end?

- *Manufacturing capabilities*   Does the product effectively use existing resources? Can current processes be modified to build the product, thereby increasing capacity utilization? Are vendors and materials easily found for needed parts and processes? Does the product pass through a bottleneck area? What is the product's projected cycle and throughput time? How do these match with current demand on the manufacturing process?

- *Part standardization*   To what extent does the product use parts that are already made or purchased by the firm? Does it use materials that the firm uses in other parts of its operations? If unique parts are required, are they easily obtainable or not?

A good design starts by developing answers to these questions before a single unit is made or dollar spent on tooling or technology. If

a design for a new product or process fails on these four dimensions—
if it has too much or too little functionality, is inflexible in design and
function, requires new, untried (and expensive) manufacturing capabilities, or uses large numbers of custom parts—the design is flawed
because it is building in waste. Only by recognizing the danger of
waste and eliminating it before any funds are spent to make a product
can a company repeatedly generate value through innovation. Eliminating waste at 3M and Toyota starts long before the product hits the
plant floor: it begins the day a design engineer or design team mem-
ber says, "What if?"

MEASURING AND ELIMINATING WASTE: KEY TO SUCCESSFUL INNOVATION

*Had I been present at the creation of the world I would have proposed
some improvements.*

ALFONSO X (4)

Measuring and eliminating waste are essential elements of effective
innovation in a company. If waste is left unrecorded and undetected, it
grows. With that fact in mind, what type of measurements can be used
to better understand the amount, type, and location of waste embedded in the design process? Four specific measurement approaches can
be used: time-to-market measures, gap measures of actual cost versus
target cost at the launch date, gap measures of actual cost versus
planned cost and profit at all stages of the product life cycle, and the
number and cost of engineering change notices.

Time Is Money—and Can Be Wasted

Time is of the essence in the design and development of new products. Competitors are always inching up on the company, trying to
come out with a better mousetrap first. And the market rewards those
who arrive in the market with a new product before anyone else. One

form of waste in the design phase, then, is *excess* time. As with all excesses, unnecessarily long development times translate to the increased use of resources.

Measuring this form of waste starts with creating a straw-man model or template of what the optimal design and development process would look like for a typical new product. This straw-man model should include both the activities that are critical to a successful launch and the points where concurrent design or parallel development efforts can be used to trim the total time required to complete the design cycle (see Figure 4.3). With this benchmark in place, a company can evaluate its current design process and time it requires. Doing this comparison results in two different waste measures—foregone profits and excess costs.

Foregone Profits. Foregone profits are the opportunity cost a company faces when it doesn't get its products to market fast enough. These opportunity costs have traditionally been considered an economic concept that couldn't be practically applied in a business setting. Why? Because traditional accounting systems can record only a cost that has actually been incurred.

Target-costing models provide an alternative framework for valuing the potential profits, and therefore foregone profits, that are caused by excessive time in the development process. What would this measurement look like?

$$\text{Actual design days} - \text{Optimal design days} = \text{Excess design days}$$

$$\frac{\text{Excess}}{\text{design days}} \times \frac{\text{Planned}}{\text{production per day}} \times \frac{\text{Target profit}}{\text{per unit}} = \frac{\text{Foregone}}{\text{profits}}$$

Foregone profits are the worst form of waste because profits are the fuel for the value-creation machine. While other forms of waste may reduce the total resources available for the next period, waste in the form of foregone profits eliminates them: nothing is there to use or to waste.

FIGURE 4.3 PARING THE WASTE IN DESIGN

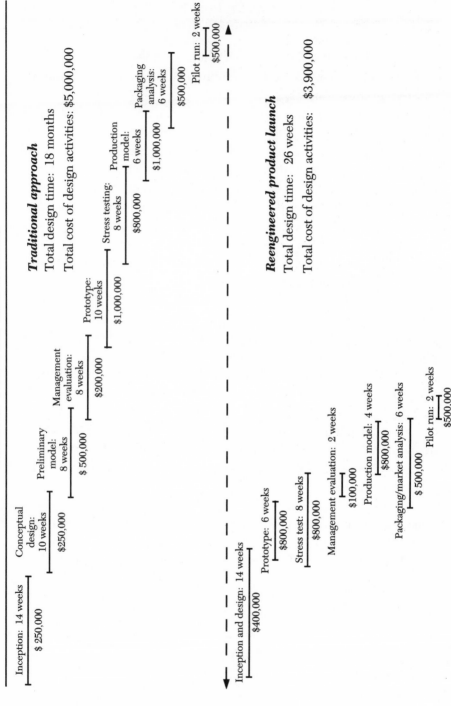

Traditional approach

Total design time: 18 months

Total cost of design activities: $5,000,000

Inception: 14 weeks — $ 250,000

Conceptual design: 10 weeks — $250,000

Preliminary model: 8 weeks — $ 500,000

Management evaluation: 8 weeks — $200,000

Prototype: 10 weeks — $1,000,000

Stress testing: 8 weeks — $800,000

Production model: 6 weeks — $1,000,000

Packaging analysis: 6 weeks — $500,000

Pilot run: 2 weeks — $500,000

Reengineered product launch

Total design time: 26 weeks

Total cost of design activities: $3,900,000

Inception and design: 14 weeks — $400,000

Prototype: 6 weeks — $800,000

Stress test: 8 weeks — $800,000

Management evaluation: 2 weeks — $100,000

Production model: 4 weeks — $800,000

Packaging/market analysis: 6 weeks — $ 500,000

Pilot run: 2 weeks — $500,000

This measurement can be developed and tracked for each new product launch. Improvement over time in terms of a lowering of foregone profits can be a good leading indicator of improved strategic positioning (assuming, of course, that the right products are being developed!). An even more powerful use of this measure, though, is in the planning process. If time is taken to evaluate the current planned launch cycle versus the straw-man benchmark *before* action is set in motion on the project, efforts can be made to eliminate this form of waste before it occurs. It is much easier for people to accept changes in the design process if the effect of these changes can be tied to the bottom-line results of the company.

Excess Costs. Excess costs in the design phase arise from a mismatch between the functionality needed in a product and the level of functionality that is built in. Excesses also can be identified if nonstandard parts are used when standard parts would do and if cumbersome activity chains and tasking are used to accomplish design work. Finally, excess costs in the development phase can be created when the effect of variety on costs is not recognized. The rule when dealing with "excesses" of this type is that the more a company can create products that fit the current structures and processes it has mastered, the lower the total cost to launch the product and the higher the total profitability of the firm.

We are all, unfortunately, familiar with debacles uncovered in the federal government, where simple wrenches end up costing $15,000. These are situations where a standard product probably would have met everyone's needs, but the intense focus on the form, rather than the function, of the product buried common sense under an avalanche of paperwork and regulations. The rules and regulations that guide design and purchasing specifications in the federal government are one of the most troubling examples of activities, tasks, and functions that waste resources and benefit no one in the long run.

What are some measurements that can be developed to track the "excesses" that create waste in the development process? While the possibilities for measurement are numerous, some of the most likely candidates are

- Theoretical cost to attain basic functionality versus design cost,
- Percentage of standard versus nonstandard parts,
- Complexity of the detailed routing,
- Degree of variety in the design and where it appears in the production process,
- Value-added cost versus total design cost,
- Ease of manufacturing and repair, and
- Opportunity cost of non-value-adding design time.

Several of these measures are easy to obtain, while others require a detailed analysis of the development process. In total, though, these measures provide a sound counterbalance to the drive to add more functionality to a product (see Figure 4.4).

The excess functionality of a product is easy to spot and measure. Simply compare the market price, or perceived value of the product or service as defined by the customer, and the price required to cover the costs of making the product. In equation form:

$$\text{Functionality gap} = \text{Market price} - \text{``Cost-plus'' price}$$

Clearly this gap measure has several factors embedded in it, such as the cost of materials, the basic elements of the design, complexity of the product and processes, and so forth, but this one measure provides a quick reality check on what a company is doing—one that is hard to argue with.

At Machine Works, this measurement served as the basis for a total redesign of the new above-ground lift. As the gap between the cost-plus price and market price was analyzed, it became clear that the

FIGURE 4.4 BALANCING DESIGN AND VALUE CREATION

The customer is buying . . .

Basic functionality

Desired level of variety

Customization

Durability

Reliability

Style and attractiveness

Image

The value created . . .

. . . but won't pay for . . .

Excesses . . .

Whether they are good features or bad, payment is based on matching the features with those demanded.

product simply was overdesigned. It looked great, but the basic functionality of raising and lowering a car had been obtained through a complex, expensive combination of hydraulics and levers. The competition used simple chain-driven mechanisms to achieve the same result.

Of course, functionality gaps can be identified in other ways. After a product is launched, customers can be asked what percentage of the product's capability they use and, more important, would be willing to pay for. Exceeding customer expectations is as problematic as falling short of them: both create waste, simply in different ways. The acid test—the dollar-driven functionality gap—focuses everyone's attention on the goal of matching customer needs.

Closing Gaps to Prevent Waste

Gaps occur whenever plans fail to become reality. Earlier in this chapter, measurements of the gap between target cost at launch and actual cost of a product at its launch were discussed (see Figure 4.3). The basic message given by these measures was clear: if a company launches its products before it achieves its target cost objectives, it will face intense pressure in the postdesign phase to cut these excess costs.

When target costs are not calculated at all, costs at launch will probably be too high. Without a cap or measure to guide their decisions and efforts, design engineers and related development professionals can unknowingly build in excess functionality or features. It's not that they purposely set out to achieve this result. It is simply that "excess" cannot be defined or measured without a benchmark target to use as a guide, as illustrated by the Machine Works example. Equipped with this tool, the design professionals can, and do, deliver a product that meets specifications without excessive cost, functionality, or features.

In addition to looking at the gap between target cost and actual cost at launch, and throughout the product life cycle, a company can examine actual versus planned profits by stage. How does this differ from target costing? Target costing is usually focused on the cost of one unit of product or service. Profitability measures, on the other hand, emphasize the total revenue and costs generated by a product or service. In other words, profit measures factor in the volume of sales achieved by a company. To measure profitability gaps, several simple calculations need to be done:

$$\begin{array}{c} \text{Market} \\ \text{price} \end{array} \times \begin{array}{c} \text{Actual volume} \\ \text{sold} \end{array} = \begin{array}{c} \text{Total actual} \\ \text{revenue} \end{array}$$

$$\begin{array}{c} \text{Market} \\ \text{price} \end{array} \times \begin{array}{c} \text{Planned sales} \\ \text{volume} \end{array} = \begin{array}{c} \text{Total target} \\ \text{revenue} \end{array}$$

$$\begin{array}{c} \text{Target cost} \\ \text{per unit} \end{array} \times \begin{array}{c} \text{Volume} \\ \text{sold} \end{array} = \begin{array}{c} \text{Total target} \\ \text{cost} \end{array}$$

Actual cost per unit $\times$ Volume sold = Total actual cost

Using these basic relationships, then, a series of measurements can be developed:

Profit potential = Target revenue − Total target cost

Revenue gap = Total target revenue − Total actual revenue

$$\frac{\text{Profit}}{\text{gap}} = \text{Profit Potential} - (\text{Actual revenue} - \text{Actual cost})$$

Volume gap = Actual revenue − Total target cost

Cost gap = Total actual cost − Total target cost

$$\frac{\text{Market}}{\text{share gap}} = \frac{\text{Actual market}}{\text{share \%}} - \frac{\text{Planned market}}{\text{share \%}}$$

Clearly, many other measures and relationships could be explored in looking for gaps in what actually takes place and what a company planned in terms of profit and costs in the design and development of its new products and services, but this set provides a comprehensive overview of what is going wrong and where. In addition, these measurements can be taken at various stages in the product life cycle, helping a company focus on its performance against their product life-cycle goals in terms of profits, costs, and market share.

The goal in developing gap measures is not to find someone to hold accountable for the "misses" but rather to help in future planning cycles. If consistent problems or shortfalls between planned market share and actual share are spotted, perhaps the solution will lie in better market research before launch, different packaging, different advertising, or different distribution channels. These questions can be asked, though, only when the waste created by current practices is identified.

Justifying an additional $25,000 of advertising is less difficult when the revenue-based benefits of doing so can be measured. And if the measurement of these relationships takes place on a regular basis, following agreed-upon practices and approaches, the "politics" can be taken out of analyzing market and manufacturing perfor-mance on new products and processes. That is the beauty of measurement. If done objectively and with attention to telling the whole story, measurements can help combat the natural tendency toward politics and power as the basis for decision making in an organization.

Engineering Change Notices: Mistakes We Can See

It is perhaps a bit harsh to call an engineering change notice a clear signal of waste or of a mistake being made, but in a world dedicated to maximizing performance through the elimination of waste, hon-esty is a requirement. The message delivered by this statement is a simple one: good people design products that sometimes fail to meet basic criteria for manufacturability, cost performance, or func-tionality. The mistakes are not intentional, but the results are a series of "re's" that chew up profits and place scarce resource "barriers" between what a company currently does and the new products and processes it would like to be able to offer its customers. Money spent to reengineer a product or process after it has been put into produc-tion creates waste at every turn—a waste that is seldom tallied or examined.

Engineering change notices (ECNs) are an anathema to everyone who has to make the new product, process, or service a reality for the customer. Rather than mastering a specific activity or process, people and departments are left struggling with revisions, rework, scrap, three (or more) different parts for the same product that may even bear the same part number, retrofitting of finished product to meet new specifications, and on and on and on. In fact, engineering change notices may create more hidden costs than any other "activity" performed in the design and development process.

How can these costs be measured? If a company has implemented activity-based costing, it is fairly easy to develop a cost for each of these "re's." Even if a company doesn't have one of the "new and improved" costing systems, though, it can easily gauge the impact of ECNs through a simple survey of everyone affected during the process of responding to an ECN. The information entered on this survey consists of estimates and perhaps even exaggerations, but the goal isn't to create a precise number or cost but rather to gain attention. That is an important fact to keep in mind when embarking on the systematic measurement of waste: *precision is not the goal; attention getting is.* As long as the numbers bear some resemblance to reality, they will serve their purpose.

The cost of ECNs, though, doesn't stop with the work done to meet these new requirements. In addition to the basic list of "re's" are the scrap created as old parts are eliminated and the increased potential for downstream errors caused by multiple drawings, parts, and potential assembly procedures. Keeping track of the revisions, the "right" set of drawings, the "right" parts, and the "right" procedures can become a full-time job—a job that prevents waste in one respect but is itself wasteful.

Finally, there are hidden costs in inventory, computer transactions, purchasing procedures, marketing and product materials provided to customers, opportunity costs as valuable time is stolen from other activities (such as driving toward continuous-improvement goals), and the potential for damaged customer relations. A company that has to retrofit its products in the field is going to raise more than a few questions in its customers' minds about the safety, reliability, and durability of the product they have bought. They may prefer the retrofit to its alternative—premature failure of the product—but in reality, they'd prefer that the company do it right the first time.

FOCUSING ATTENTION ON THE CAUSES OF COST

The man who does not go down to underlying causes will never get at the heart of evil.

HENRI DE LUBAC
Paradoxes (1)

Designing a new product, service, or process is the most crucial step in the value chain that creates long-term value for customers and long-term survival for a company. The design locks in over 90 percent of the total cost of the product: very little can be done downstream to eliminate the effect of a poor design and the costs it causes. A product that is overdesigned does not create value; it creates waste. A product that is misdesigned does not save money; it throws it away. In the search for a better mousetrap, the goal is to create products and processes that meet customer expectations and yield a profit for the company. A company that loses money every time it sells an overdesigned or overly complicated product cannot make up the loss with volume. A statement of this fact is usually greeted with a knowing smile and chuckle from a businessperson, but an honest review of what really takes place in most companies turns the comedy into a tragedy.

Why measure waste in the design phase? Measuring performance in the design phase focuses attention on this vital link in the value-creation process. If mistakes are made early in the life cycle, before a customer ever sees a product or benefits from a service, life-cycle profits may be reduced. If these mistakes are left unaddressed until full-scale production is under way, the company will never be able to recoup these losses in the highly competitive global marketplace. Shrinking life cycles and intense pressure on prices have made the traditional high-profit period immediately following the launch of a new product into the marketplace a myth.

As fast as a company can design and build a new product, its competition can match the effort. Patent protection cannot be relied on in the global marketplace: the rules of the game change as one leaves the borders of the United States. A company has to assume, right out of the gate, that it is going to be restricted to a "fair and reasonable" profit for its efforts. This fact places increased pressure and emphasis on getting products to market quickly by doing things right the first time.

So why measure waste in the design phase? First, this ensures that this area receives high priority in a company. Future profits are driven by product design and development. The cost of doing this task poorly is not only reduced profits in the short run; it is the danger of failure in the long term. A second reason for measuring waste in this area is more pointed: developing a cost estimate of the waste created by ECNs, nonstandard part utilization, and the other *controllable and avoidable* costs caused in the design phase makes it possible to hold individuals and departments accountable for their performance in this area.

The ability to hold people accountable for results is a key element in driving behavioral change in an organization. While it may sound a bit old fashioned to talk about accountability in a modern "empowered" organization, individuals who know what their goals are and what is expected of them will be more likely to accomplish those goals. It is not fair to groan and mutter about the impact of ECNs and to denigrate the value of the design team without first making the criteria for success in this area clear. Providing design teams with a clear set of goals increases their chance of success.

In the end, what matters is not only what is measured *but how and why those measurements are used.* If any of the waste measurements suggested in this book are used as a "hammer" to beat people into performing as management dictates, dysfunctional behavior will occur. The reason for this is simple: for every control tool or measure that a company develops, employees can find at least one way to circumvent the measurement.

The goal is not to control behavior but to focus attention on the areas of waste that are hurting the company and putting at risk the long-term survival of the organization (and, therefore, the jobs of the people who work there). *Measuring and eliminating waste are the secret to long-term success but if and only if it is used to help an organization learn to do things better, faster, and cheaper.* Learning is the ultimate goal—not control.

The new circumstances under which we are placed call for new words, new phrases, and for the transfer of old words to new objects.

THOMAS JEFFERSON (2)

CHAPTER 5

Truth or Consequences

Logical consequences are the scarecrows of fools and the beacons of wise men.

THOMAS H. HUXLEY
Animal Automatism (7)

The most difficult part about making decisions is that all their potential consequences cannot be determined at the start. While hindsight may be 20-20, foresight is unavoidably flawed. Without a crystal ball to guide them as well as the ability to respond almost immediately to unforeseen events, companies and the managers who direct them are constantly staring risk in the face. All decisions are risky, even the decision to not make a decision. But how can we use the concepts of waste or potential waste to help pinpoint the risk of a specific decision or course of action?

The answer to this question lies in the basic statement about organizational life that underlies this entire book: *you get what you measure and reward.* This comment cannot be made too often; it is the subliminal message that has been built into every figure, diagram, and example used in these pages. Following on the heels of this "factoid," though, is a second key idea: *honesty in measurement is not a virtue; it is a necessity.*

What is an honest measure? It is one that spells out the good with the bad, that starts with an estimate of the best you can be and compares where you are to where you want to go. An honest measure lays out the gaps and the causes of those gaps in objective terms. An honest measure does not seek to attach blame but rather to support learning through analysis and continuous improvement. In other words, achieving the power of measurement for changing behavior and focusing attention starts with objective, complete, and accurate assessments of current state and desired future events.

Another way to think about the concepts presented in this chapter is to recognize that if the numbers used to support a decision or to evaluate performance are flawed, so is any action or subsequent decision that is made based on this information. Bad measurements are the worst form of "garbage in—garbage out" because they are used over and over again and often form the basis for new standards and new goals. It's no easier to build a sound measurement system on faulty numbers than it is to build a house on sand. A solid foundation is the key to long-term usefulness in information systems.

In this chapter the focus turns, then, toward the waste that is created by the "games" companies play when budgeting. Based more on politics and power than facts in many cases, this planning tool can create chaos downstream unless it is built on honest, objective assessments of the current performance of the organization, the benefits of alternative paths for improvement, and accurate feedback of actual performance against these plans. Budgets are central to organizational life; to remain central in the long term they have to be based on honest measurements and not politics.

WHEN THE RUBBER MEETS THE ROAD:
AVOIDABLE VERSUS AVOIDED COSTS

It is always a relief to believe what is pleasant, but it is more important to believe what is true.

HILAIRE BELLOC
The Silence of the Sea (1)

Waste can be created in many different ways in a company. In the capital-budgeting area, for instance, waste is embedded in the assumptions used to make the decision, the criteria used to determine whether to fund a specific project, and the way promised savings are verified after the project has been approved and implemented. Capital budgeting can, in fact, turn into a sort of shell game in a company unless the difference between avoidable and avoided costs is understood and used. The goal is to ensure that the capital assets purchased really deliver more value than they consume in terms of other company resources, lost opportunities, and future profit potential.

What is an *avoidable cost?* It is a cost that will, or could, *go away* if a decision is made or a course of action followed. For instance, if a company outsources its payroll function, it should be able to avoid all the internal costs of doing this type of work: people, space, equipment, and supplies should all be eliminated if the complete benefits of the outsourcing decision are to be reaped. An *avoided cost*, then, is the real saving a company experiences from the outsourcing decision. *The difference between the avoidable and avoided costs is a gap measure that can be used to judge the effectiveness of a capital-budgeting decision.* As this gap increases, more waste is being added to the total costs of doing business for the company. This is because an unavoided cost translates to the use of excess resources in completing an activity or operating a process.

The Capital-Budgeting Game

The essence of capital budgeting is the estimation of future cash flows generated by or used by the new asset, process, or plant. This "game" is defined around a set of assumptions and rules, including the following:

1. Cash today is worth more to us than cash tomorrow.

2. While important, fuzzy qualitative factors are harder to include in the decision process than their "harder" cousins, quantitative cash-flow measures.

3. Future cash flows can be projected with some degree of certainty.

4. The cash flows caused by the project in question can be separated from the cash flows that are created by other activities, products, projects, and processes.

5. Labor savings include savings in the overhead that go with those labor dollars or labor hours.

6. It is always better to substitute machines for men.

7. Automation is, in itself, a good thing.

8. The asset being acquired will generate the promised savings, even if these savings can't be measured.

9. Everyone is being honest about the numbers they create.

10. The "game" is based on objective facts and not politics or opinions.

The list could be made longer, but the message is clear as it stands: capital budgeting *is* a game that follows prescribed rules that define how the numbers are created, evaluated, and used. But what do the underlying numbers really say?

If the fluff is cut away from the capital-budgeting process and the cash flows it relies on, the "dicey" numbers that remain may or may not come to pass. First, it is almost impossible to accurately project the future cash flows caused by, and only by, one specific project or new capital asset. An organization creates value and generates its cash flows by using many different resources over the course of making a product or providing a service. To attempt to isolate the benefits of one specific piece of this value-creation process is simply not logical: if it could be done, would the benefits exceed the costs?

Why focus on the benefits of one asset when what matters is whether the process, in total, has improved its performance? Focusing on one asset and its effects, in fact, can actually increase the total cost of the process. The reason behind this seemingly illogical conclusion is that the only addition to a process that matters is one that addresses a bottleneck or removes a major problem that is negatively affecting the effectiveness of the process. In the complex, interrelated world of business, the performance of the whole system, not the performance of one machine or one person, has to be optimized.

Measures can be developed at the process level to evaluate the effect of a new asset on total profitability, as suggested in Figure 5.1. For each of these measures, the underlying question being addressed is whether the entire company benefited from the decision. The alternative, of course, is that waste was created instead. Did total costs per good unit produced go down? Did quality go up? Did throughput time drop? Is the process more flexible than before? Is capacity utilization up? These are the factors that define the effectiveness of a capital-budgeting decision.

Are the savings real? If a systemic view is taken, are all the potential pitfalls of the capital-budgeting process avoided? Not really. Savings realized in one process, even if it is a complete system, may not mean that the company as a whole is better off. There are several reasons for this problem. First, many of the projected "savings" are based on eliminating people from the organization—labor cost reductions. But seldom do people really "go away." Instead, the company ends up shifting the displaced workers to another part of the company, where

FIGURE 5.1 MEASURING NEW ASSET IMPACTS

Impact on total costs

$$\frac{\text{Change in total costs after purchase}}{\text{Original total costs}} = \text{Profit improvement \%}$$

This should be positive.

$$\frac{\begin{array}{c}\text{Cost per good unit}\\\text{produced after asset purchase}\end{array}}{\begin{array}{c}\text{Cost per good unit produced before}\\\text{asset purchase}\end{array}} = \text{Cost performance}$$

This should be less than 1.

Impact on quality

$$\frac{\text{Change in piece part per million defect rate}}{\text{Original defect rate (PPM)}} = \text{Quality improvement \%}$$

This should be positive.

$$\frac{\text{Total cost of quality before asset purchase}}{\text{Total cost of quality after asset purchase}} = \text{Quality performance}$$

This should be less than 1.

Impact on the process

$$\frac{\text{Change in throughput time}}{\text{Original throughput time}} = \text{Throughput time improvement \%}$$

This should be positive.

$$\frac{\text{Setup time after asset purchase}}{\text{Setup time before asset purchase}} = \text{Flexibility metric}$$

This should be greater than 1.

$$\frac{\text{Capacity utilization before asset purchase}}{\text{Capacity utilization after asset purchase}} = \text{Capacity utilization improvement percentage}$$

This should be greater than 1.

96

they may or may not perform value-adding work. The result of this "shell-game" approach to implementing projects is that the company, in total, ends up with the same number of people it had in the first place and even more fixed assets. More cost is generated with little additional value created for the company's customers.

Do people purposely lie about the projected savings a project offers? No, they don't. In fact, the real villain behind this shell game is the performance-evaluation process that holds individuals accountable for the results in their area only. When the decision is made to implement an improvement in one area, there is little or no recognition or concern for the cost shifting that takes place in the company as a whole. As Table 5.1 suggests, the result of this myopic approach is predictable: total costs go up, waste proliferates, and profits disappear from view.

There are several ways this game can be uncovered and derailed. First, if a head-count reduction is promised, it must take place based on the *total number* of employees that work in the firm. If the total number of people, or total resources, used by the company actually goes up after the "cost savings" project is implemented, this failure to meet project goals has to be identified and assigned directly to the area that originally fostered the idea. This may sound like control, the demon that can erode motivation and create dysfunctional behavior, but the alternative is the proliferation of a game that is equally, if not more, destructive in total. Clearly, Ford Motor Company believes that the promised savings should appear. As noted earlier, these savings are used to reduce the allowable production cost (or standard) the day that the new asset is put into use. If twenty-five cents are supposed to be saved on every unit produced with a new piece of equipment, twenty-five cents will be removed from the allowable cost standard as soon as that asset is put on line.

Recognizing that not every cost saving can be attained rapidly, a company can track its total cost per good unit produced over time, noting whether the sum total of the projects has yielded the desired downward trend in total costs. This isn't a perfect measure, but it keeps everyone's eyes focused on the enterprise or business unit's

TABLE 5.1 THE CAPITAL BUDGETING GAME

Department A's cost

	Before the asset purchase	*After* the asset purchase
Materials	$ 250.00	$ 250.00
Labor	100.00	25.00
Machine costs	200.00	225.00
Indirect charges	100.00	100.00
Overhead	400.00	100.00
Total product cost	$1,050.00	$ 700.00

What looks like a cost savings at the department level is actually a cost increase for the company.

Total company costs

	Before the asset purchase	*After* the asset purchase
Materials	$ 5,000,000	$ 5,000,000
Labor	1,500,000	1,750,000
Machine costs	8,000,000	9,000,000
Indirect charges	1,500,000	1,500,000
Overhead	7,500,000	8,000,000
Total Product Cost	$23,500,000	$ 25,250,000

Why?

The costs aren't really avoided: they're shifted to other parts of the company!

performance. The message embedded in any of these measurement options is that *whatever is promised in the capital-budgeting proposal has to happen.* If it doesn't, capital budgeting becomes a game. Games may be fun, but they are hardly productive in a business setting.

To Audit or Not to Audit

Are all capital-budgeting decisions the same? In a medium-sized Pennsylvania company producing watch and timing components for various types of weaponry, this question was answered with a re-sounding no. As described by the company president:

> *We came to the realization that not every decision we make in this area is the same. Some decisions were no-brainers. If we didn't replace the machine or change the process, the EPA or some other group would shut us down, or we'd simply be unable to continue producing in this plant at all. What was to cost justify? The downside of the decision was to go out of business. That seemed like an unacceptable alternative to us. In a similar way, some of the decisions we were making were based on hopes and dreams, perhaps, but we felt they were an essential part of building our future. If we tried to create cash flows around these decisions, we'd be making them up. That didn't make a lot of sense either. So we decided that we wouldn't use the traditional capital-budgeting tools for these decisions. The only ones that we use these tools on today are the replacement decisions—we already have the machine or process going, and we need to replace one machine or one part of the system to either maintain it or to improve its performance. If we can't put accurate cash flows on these, we shouldn't be in business. Period.*

The moral of this story is that different types of investment decisions need to be approached and justified in very different ways. *Survival*-driven decisions—such as placing scrubbers inside of the smoke-stacks of a paper mill to cut down on the emission of sulfur and other chemicals—are not optional. The only decision that can be made is to make the investment. The alternative is to close the doors, shut off the lights, and go home.

Growth-based decisions, on the other hand, present major challenges to anyone trying to apply traditional capital-budgeting tools. What future cash flows will be created by the decision? Some may be known, and others estimated, but no one can argue that these numbers are firm. Many of the cash outflows caused by the decision can be tracked, but what about the inflows? Not only are they intertwined with all of the inflows caused by all of the other decisions made along the way, they are also based, themselves, on a series of assumptions and guesses.

Putting cash inflow numbers on growth-based asset decisions is like pounding sand: you may get rid of a bit of frustration, but the risk has not gone away. Growth decisions are risky. They are also essential to long-term survival of the company. Once management has passed the "We think this is a good way for the company to go" hurdle, its focus has to turn toward making these new projects, processes, or products a success. Worrying about accurately projecting future cash flows is not the issue: obtaining the future cash flows is.

The final class of capital-budgeting problem falls under the classification of *replacement* decisions. A replacement decision is the simplest of all. The company is already doing the work, and perhaps even using a machine to do it, and the only question is whether to buy a new asset to replace the old. Why would this be done? A logical reason would be that the asset is worn out. It may be constantly breaking down or perhaps have already given up the ghost: it has to be replaced.

Another reason for replacing assets might be that a new technology has been developed that is so superior to what the company currently has that it makes sense to replace the old machines with the new. There's a catch here, of course. If the new technology can perform at a much higher level than the rest of the machines, people, and processes that make up the value-creation system, its purchase is not a good idea: it is waste.

Finally, a machine may have been identified that can "replace" direct labor. These replacement decisions are the diciest of all. First, while a machine may be faster than people, it is not as flexible. Only if the machine performs better than people on many dimensions should it be put in place. Fixed assets don't go away if volumes drop, product mix shifts, or other events transpire to change the workflow. People, flexible as they are, can either "go away" in one-person chunks or be redeployed rapidly to new activities or new products. Second, when investment decisions are based on labor savings (plus their overhead), the people must go away. Otherwise the decision is faulty: rather than saving money it is creating waste.

Identifying and eliminating waste in the capital-budgeting game starts with recognizing that not all decisions are equal and ends with making sure that promised savings appear. No one gains if a decision is justified using shaky numbers, questionable assumptions, and inadequate knowledge; waste is the only possible outcome here. In addition, when a decision is made to buy a machine to replace a person, the only cost that will go away is the salary paid to the worker. Overhead won't go away: it will actually go up because the cost of the fixed asset is added to overhead in most situations. This may sound like a technicality, but the result is not: overhead rates in the plant go up, and every product made there is negatively affected.

The key to making effective capital-budgeting decisions is to understand the type of decisions they are, to apply decision criteria that fit the situation at hand, and to do after-the-fact audits of the benefits really provided by the new product, project, process, or asset. If an asset was purchased because it is faster and more accurate than the asset it replaces, its effect *on the system* should be measured. Looking at the asset's performance from any other perspective hides the waste that may exist. In the final analysis, the goal is to match the promised benefits with those really attained—to audit the project using measurements and criteria that fit the situation at hand.

HITTING THE TARGET AND
OTHER INTERESTING FABLES

*To be absolutely certain about something, one must know everything or
nothing about it.*

OLIN MILLER (4)

Capital budgeting isn't the only type of estimating that goes on in
Western companies. In fact, capital budgeting is usually performed
only one time a year, is driven by top management, and is constrained
by the projected cash available from all of the other value-creating
activities a company performs. Capital budgeting is clearly not the only
game in town. What other games abound? The annual budgeting
process may be the biggest game of all. The goal of the game is to
secure as many resources as possible for your area and to promise the
least amount of performance possible to get these resources. While this
may sound a bit cynical, the problem is that the games that have been
built up around traditional budgeting cycles are among the most
waste-creating activities a company undertakes.

What are the problems in the budgeting process, and how do they
create waste? To start with, budgets are normally *incremental*: next
year's spending limit is last year's limit plus some designated percentage or dollar-based increase (see Figure 5.2). That means that any
waste that was present in the prior budget remains, and more is added
on top. The result is more waste than value creation. Once this point is
hit, a company usually goes into the "cost-reduction" mode of operation, cutting funds indiscriminately across the board. The result is a
double whammy for those managers and areas foolish enough to
budget carefully in the first place: they lose current funds to lose
future funds. In addition, since the cost-reduction process is unfocused, good activities and people get cut with the bad, which creates
even more waste in total.

FIGURE 5.2 BUILDING WASTE THROUGH INCREMENTAL BUDGETING

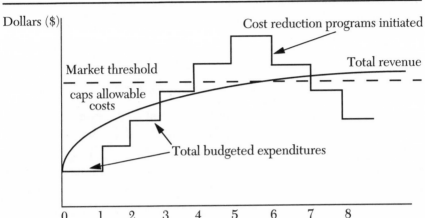

When budgets grow incrementally, they result in layers of waste. As companies attempt to pass these excess costs through to the market, they eventually exceed the customer's "value" assessment for the good or service. The result is plummeting profits, which then leads to across-the-board cost reduction programs. This vicious cycle can be stopped only by measuring and eliminating waste on an ongoing basis.

The ways that waste is built into a company through the budgeting process include

- "Budget creep" or the incremental growth of cost and waste;

- "Tight but attainable" budget targets that are anything but tight;

- The "spend it or lose it" approach to annual budgets;

- "You'uns versus us'ns" or the effect of functional budgets that all but ignore the underlying value-creation process;

- "Pass the variance" or evaluations that aren't;

- "If only the forecasts were right" and other divisive tales;

- "We need more resources" and other pleas; and

- Confusing means with ends or the "Why are we doing this anyway?" debate.

These are the issues that define a traditional budgeting process. While they have been placed in a gaming framework, the result of the unchecked growth of waste created by the budgeting process is anything but a game. What can be done about these games?

Budget Creep: Adding Inches to the Waste Line

Budget creep is the natural result of annual budgeting approaches that don't begin by asking, "Are we doing the right things?" Rather than evaluating the amount of value created by a set of resources, companies rely on past spending patterns and the persuasiveness of their managers to divvy up the corporate pie. Budgets, done incrementally across functional areas, are not good planning tools. They are, instead, spending limits. What is negotiated during the budget process is the percentage of the company's scarce resources that any one department or function is going to get: value creation is seldom, if ever, broached in these discussions.

If you think about it, it is easy to see how and why incremental budgeting was developed and also why it creates excessive waste. The how and why issues revolve around the sheer complexity of trying to sit down once a year and actually figure out who is doing what, why, and where. While it is one thing to "company speak" value creation and meeting customer expectations, it is much harder to identify the core set of activities that make up this competency. It is easier to look at prior spending patterns, adjust a bit for new programs or the downsizing of old ones, and trust that people will do the right thing when the time comes. So why do incremental budgeting? Zero-based, or from scratch, budgets are time consuming and quite likely waste creating.

That leaves the issue of waste unaddressed, though. Why does waste proliferate in the budgeting process? Because the company never assigns resources directly to the processes and subsystems that create value for the customer, it cannot ferret out good spending from bad spending. The initial step in any budgeting process should be an assessment of the effectiveness of the value-creation process, the clear definition of the existing value chains that make the products or deliver the services, and a prioritization of activities and spending based on where the biggest bang for the buck (in terms of improved customer satisfaction or increased systemic efficiency) will be. In other words, sound budgets are based on value chains and not prior spending.

The target-costing model presented earlier provides a basis for developing measures around the effectiveness of the budget process. But how can a company migrate from incremental budgets to budgets that focus on value creation and the elimination of waste? The first step is to detail the value chains that underlie the work done in the organization. The second step is to attempt to match the resources spent to these chains. The third step is to evaluate current spending by activity against a list of prioritized spending goals. The result is a gap measure of spending effectiveness (see Figure 5.3).

An approach used by Stratus Computer, a Boston-based producer of fail-safe computer backup systems, provides an alternative way to begin squeezing waste out of the budgeting process. As described by Mark Boissonneault, a company spokesperson, requests for increased budgets or for a continuation of current funding are denied. That sounds a bit simplistic, but the way that the company operationalizes its view of budgets is not.

When a manager asks for additional resources at Stratus, he or she is asked to first look at the current workload and search for ways that these activities can be done better, faster, and cheaper. The result of this approach on one area of the company, the quality department, was marked. New products, processes, and reliability levels had been developed during the year, leading to increased demands for certain types of tests in the quality area. The manager of this area felt that he couldn't possibly keep up with the higher demand for tests without adding at least one more high-level engineer to his staff. Armed with what he perceived to be a legitimate request, the manager went to his budget meeting ready to ask for and receive more resources.

The asking took place; the granting of resources did not. Instead, Mark asked this manager to look at the work his lab was currently doing and see if any of the procedures could be streamlined to

FIGURE 5.3 SPENDING EFFECTIVENESS: COST CONTAINMENT IN ACTION

Step One: Detail the value chain. | **Mail Order Business**

Customer calls in order	Inventory and credit check done on-line	Order processed and packing slip printed	Items picked by store room	Backorders noted with expected shipping dates	Order packed	Box sealed and labeled	Box weighed and paper-work done	Moved to pick-up area	Ship to customer	Invoice	Collect cash

Step Two: Attach resources to the activities and then evaluate these spending levels against customer-defined value.

Activity	Annual Resources Used	% of Total	Customer Value
1. Answer phone	$ 25,000	less that 1%	1 (= key activity)
2. Take order and check credit and inventory	500,000	11.6%	1
3. Process order and send to storeroom	150,000	3.5%	3 (= low value)
4. Pick items on order	750,000	17.4%	1
5. Note backorders and expected ship dates	750,000	17.4%	2 (= low value; want done right)
6. Pack order	500,000	11.6%	1
7. Seal and label box	125,000	2.9%	2
8. Weigh and complete paperwork	125,000	2.9%	3
9. Move	75,000	1.7%	4 (= no value)
10. Ship	500,000	11.6%	1
11. Invoice	350,000	8.1%	2
12. Collect cash	450,000	10.5%	2

Step Three: Determine the spending gap.

Total resources used: $4,300,000

% spent on priority 1 activities: $2,275,000/$4,300,000= 53%

Desired spending on priority 1 activities: 60%, or $2,580,000

Spending gap: 7%, or $305,000

eliminate unnecessary activities, time, and resources. Skeptical at first, the quality manager went along with the request. After asking for process-improvement suggestions and other input from the professionals in his area, the quality manager found out that over 25 percent of the workload was unnecessary, cumbersome, or unnecessarily complex. He didn't need more resources to meet the new demands for testing. Instead, the department needed to eliminate unnecessary work. It did, and the demand for new resources in the area was dropped. Waste was eliminated, providing a basis for doing more work with the same amount of spending. That's a productivity improvement a company can take to the bank.

If a company wants to know how much waste it has in its processes, a simple benchmark is to count back the number of years since the last major cost-reduction drive took place, take that "tight" budget level as a starting point, and add 5 percent to this budget for each year that passes. At the end of five years, it is quite likely that the company has built in 20 to 25 percent more waste into its processes. This creeping waste, which should have been checked in the first place using the logic displayed by Stratus Computer, now becomes the target of another round of cost reductions, which continue until this 20 to 25 percent waste is squeezed back out.

It's a great game. Add waste on one end, then squeeze it out on the other. The problem is, however, that often the value-adding parts of the organization are squeezed as hard as, if not harder than, the non-value-adding parts. Waste is not defined by spending limits: it is defined by the lack of value creation. That means that the traditional incremental budgeting-cost-reduction cycle (see Figure 5.4) is pointless at best and destructive at worst. It is pointless because it fails to ask the key question: Are we doing the right things?

This returns us to the core issue. The only way a budget can be effectively developed and used is if it reflects the value-creation process. A tight budget is one that projects the theoretically best performance level for the value-adding activities (minimum cost and minimum waste for maximum value created) and allows absolutely no money for any other activity. Clearly, this isn't an attainable budget or

FIGURE 5.4 THE VALUE SQUEEZE

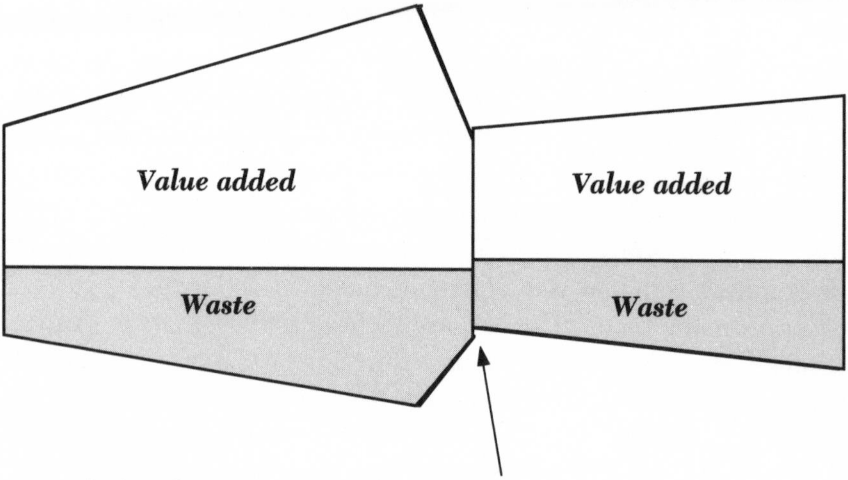

Across-the-board spending cuts squeeze out value along with waste.

one that could support the company in the long term, but it does set the baseline for spending. This baseline activity level is what the customer is buying. If more value can be created at this level, revenues and profits will increase. But if this value-adding core of activities is indiscriminately cut away in an unfocused cost-reduction process, everyone loses. By shrinking the level of expenditure on the value-adding core below an acceptable level, revenues decrease (customers have less to value), costs and waste remain unbalanced, and profits go down. The only difference between the "death spiral" approach to budgeting and the "growth spiral" method is a clear focus on value creation and not spending limits.

The Budget Paradox or the Effect of Mixing Planning with Control

The first set of issues surrounding budgets reflects a concern with effectiveness. A second concern arises from the *budget paradox*: A planning tool cannot be an effective control tool. Asking someone to be honest in their goal setting—when they know that they are going to held accountable for reaching this target—is illogical. What is the motivation for setting goals that are hard to attain? If managers set a stretch target for a year and fail, the heavy hand of control clamps down in the form of poor evaluations that can haunt them throughout their careers. With an "easy" target, the manager wins on a personal level. The downside, of course, is that the organization loses as waste is created or potential profits foregone.

A recent study by Ken Merchant[1] found that most budget targets are felt to be attainable at least 80 percent of the time. In other words, a "tight" budget is one that is almost guaranteed to be achieved. This 80 percent achievement level appears to be built into the budget at the basic assumption level, is never questioned, and (thanks to the incremental budgeting approach that was common to the companies studied) is never uncovered by management. The "game" is to ensure that everyone wins. A gentleman's sport of sorts, the budgeting process detailed by Merchant ensures that waste will be created and that personal risk will be all but eliminated.

At a multinational company in the New England area, the illogical behavior created by the budget paradox was even more profound. Instead of using budget variances as a control tool, the company was actually budgeting variances. This could be seen as a way to drive the continuous-improvement model into the budgeting process, but that didn't happen in this company. Instead, budgeted variances set the limit on the "misses" any one area could have. If this limit was exceeded, a new game called "pass the variance" was put in motion.

What was the essence of this game? At the end of a reporting period, the divisional manager sat down with all his managers and determined who had a positive variance (spent less than budget) and who had a negative one. The managers with negative variances were then allowed to "pass" their variance off to a manager with a positive variance, netting the total variances in the division to zero. The driving force behind this game was the control element of the budgeting process. Since exceeding spending limits was seen to be a sign of poor management skills, everyone focused their attention on avoiding variances and not on doing the right things or eliminating the waste that the variances represented.

Another game caused by the budget paradox and found in many companies is the "flavor of the month" excuse list. The essence of this game is that the books of the company are closed, accounting discovers that there is a variance or difference between budgeted and actual performance, and the game is afoot. Armed with the variance report, the accountant approaches the plant or departmental manager and asks for an explanation of the variance. The question is logical but impossible to answer. A thousand events occur in the course of a month—some that improve performance against budget, others that diminish it. Sorting out which one event "caused" the variance is simply not possible. But because the plant manager knows that an answer is expected, he reviews the list of "explanations" everyone seems to accept and picks one that hasn't been used in a while, the accountant dutifully writes it down, and everyone is happy.

Some plant managers are so straightforward about this game that they will pull open a drawer and hand you the list of excuses they found will work, describing how they choose which excuse to use in any specific setting. This explanation, though, is seldom accompanied by a chuckle or a note of victory of the wise (the plant manager) over the foolish (the accountant). Instead, most plant managers hate this game. What they want is information that helps them avoid problems before they happen, that sends up a red flag as soon as a crisis begins and that can help them focus on the best plan of action to arrest the problem before it gets out of hand. Finding out six weeks later that a variance was created is of no help at all. The information is too late, too aggregated, and too unfocused to really help the plant improve its performance. The plant manager knows this fact and knows that it is essential to manage what is happening right now—not to try to figure out what happened last month.

"Pass the variance," "flavor of the month," and the "tight but attainable" games that surround budgeting accomplish nothing. But they be stopped by focusing everyone's attention on identifying and eliminating waste in every activity, process, and product. The goal of this system is not control: it is decision support and planning. As Stratus Computer has discovered, controlling costs is much more productive than trying to cut them back later. The power of budgets comes up front, when the effectiveness of the company's processes is questioned. When control is bundled with the planning element of budgeting, all that a company ends up with is a new game and more waste.

Instead of variances, a company needs to develop measures that reflect the overall performance levels of the company. Budgeted goals should be stated in terms of improvement and not spending limits. Any increase in spending for an activity or an area should be closely examined to find ways to cut waste rather than add it through budget creep. What are some measures that can help a company achieve these objectives?

- $Budget\ creep\ = \dfrac{\text{Percentage increase in spending}}{\text{Percentage increase in revenues}}$

This measure can be used by department, by activity, or for the company in total. The minimum goal is zero creep. The optimal goal is to drive spending down.

- $Value\ added\ = \dfrac{\text{Planned spending for value-adding activities}}{\text{Percentage planned total spending}}$

This measure should be trended over time. The goal is to see this number trend up—more dollars dedicated to value creation and less to waste.

- $Continuous\ improvement\ = \dfrac{\text{Planned spending}}{\text{Actual spending}}$

This measure should always be less than 1. Even if slack is built into the budget, this measure will force it out. It can be applied at the various levels but must be coupled with the knowledge that the ultimate goal is to meet customer requirements.

Measures that focus on the pattern of spending over a period of time are better control tools that those that look at one department for one period. In addition, these measures have to be supported by a planning process that helps everyone focus on the effectiveness of the organization in meeting customer expectations and not on who is spending what. The only objective framework for evaluating a budget is how well it motivates people to meet customer requirements and to strive for continuous improvement. The goal is not to set minimal performance levels or static performance targets but to encourage everyone to find and eliminate waste.

THE POLITICS OF WASTE

When everyone "games" the numbers, change the measurement system to change the games.

RICHARD A. MORAN (7)

The basis of budgeting, whether it is for capital assets or operating funds, is the key to its impact on the organization. If the planning process is a game, the behavior it creates will reflect this game—its rules, objectives, and scoring system. While games may be an unavoidable part of organizational life, they should at least point everyone in the right direction—toward eliminating waste rather than promoting its growth.

The politics of waste that accompanies budgets goes beyond the numbers, though, to reflect the core values of the organization. If budgets are used solely as a way to attach blame to "guilty" parties who let the team down, they create dysfunctional behavior. Instead of promoting teamwork, this approach strengthens the functional boundaries and increases the level of friction associated with mistakes and crisis. No one wants to be found guilty, and everyone wants to be the hero. In a culture of "blame," the goal isn't to continuously improve; it is to cover your rear end when things go poorly and take credit when they go well. Whether described as a culture of "blame" or one of "heroes," the implications of this excessive focus on individual accountabilities is that staying out of trouble becomes more important than doing the right thing.

Therein lies the key to turning around the destructive games that often accompany budgets. If the games are created by the budget paradox and the individual accountabilities it creates, refocus the budget on planning for improvement at the process or business-unit level. Drop individual accountabilities for results. Recognize that one person or one department can't make a result happen—the entire organization is tied to the value-creation process. Whether people like it or not, they are in the boat together. That is the message the budgeting process has to reinforce.

Measuring the level of waste in existing processes, identifying the level of value added throughout the organization, and finding ways to eliminate waste before it is built into incremental budgets are the basis for setting up a productive budgeting process. The focus has to be on doing the right things, knowing what they are, increasing the resources dedicated to creating value and minimizing those dedicated to non-value-adding activities, putting a stop to the spending rather than later trying to reverse budget creep, and ensuring that people are not encouraged to use resources they do not really need.

The "use it or lose it" approach to budgeting is the ultimate game. It is the basis for waste everywhere it is practiced. Driven by the need to hold on to their share of the organization's scarce resources, managers in these settings may plan rationally but spend to protect their turf. The result of this game is the tangled bureaucracy and unbridled growth of spending and waste that practically defines the federal government in the United States. When politics rules the planning process, waste, not value creation, is the result.

The moral of the story? Long-term survival and growth are based on honest, accurate, objective numbers that clearly identify waste and motivate everyone to continuously improve. The goal is not to eliminate people but to eliminate non-value-adding work and the resources it consumes. If non-value-added work is cut away, resources are freed up to support an increase in value-adding work. This is a cycle of growth that doesn't result in downsizing; it results in controlled, steady growth. The time to control costs is before the money is spent and not after. In the end, it all boils down to rule number one: you get what you measure and reward.

I never give them hell. I just tell the truth and they think it's hell.

HARRY S. TRUMAN (2)

CHAPTER 6

Idle Equipment, Idle Minds

I like work: it fascinates me. I can sit and look at it for hours. I love to keep it by me; the idea of getting rid of it nearly breaks my heart.

JEROME K. JEROME
Three Men in a Boat (7)

When walking into a plant and seeing an idle worker, the first thing that most people think is, "Someone better find something for that guy to do!" It's as if nature abhors a body at rest. Idleness is not seen as a virtue: it is a socially defined waste of time and resources that most people agree is undesirable. While it is easy to locate idle people and idle equipment, it is not always logical to put these resources to work—not if the work they end up doing is waste. Trading one form of waste for another is never a solution.

As opposed as management is to idleness and the waste it represents, there are seldom any measures of this "nonactivity" in most companies' reporting systems. Without these measurements, it is hard to decide when an asset should be kept busy and when it should be allowed to sit idle. The approach of management to this issue simply becomes "Idleness is evil. Keep everyone busy." Rarely does anyone ask whether the activity creates value. Focusing solely on efficiency, managers find themselves pushing people and machines to their limits to do something, whether or not it is an effective use of the resource's capacity.

In this chapter, the focus turns toward defining and measuring capacity, identifying and measuring idle capacity, and discussing the difference between idleness and wasted resources (both human and machine). The goal is to turn around the myth that idleness is always waste and that keeping people and machines busy always creates value. Understanding the actual value-creating abilities of men and machines requires a careful analysis and measurement of all of the varied forms of waste idleness may represent and the tradeoffs inherent in managing processes to eliminate waste.

WASTE AND THE BASICS OF CAPACITY MEASUREMENT

I conceive that the great part of the miseries of mankind are brought upon them by false estimates they have made of the value of things.

BENJAMIN FRANKLIN (4)

Capacity, or a company's *capability to do work,* is normally defined around the fixed assets the company has at its disposal. How much work can a company do if it uses every process effectively, balances its production process, properly trains and motivates its employees, and ensures a steady stream of materials (raw materials, paper, or electronic transactions are all materials) to move through the system? That is its potential, or *theoretical,* capacity (see Figure 6.1). Theoretical capacity is the best baseline measure of the amount of value an organization can create.

Motorola uses theoretical capacity at the cell level to provide an objective evaluation basis for how well the cell is performing. Since a just-in-time (JIT) cell is designed around the concept of a balanced,

FIGURE 6.1 DEFINITIONS OF CAPACITY

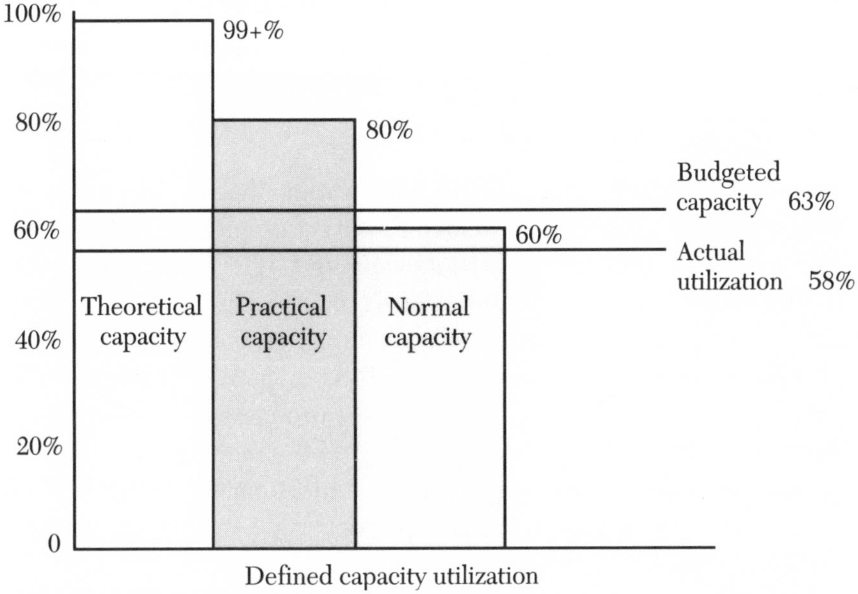

Defined capacity utilization

linear flow of materials, theoretical capacity can be both defined and measured. To track continuous improvement, then, Motorola keeps track of actual production in terms of good units produced and total productive time. The gap between current performance levels and theoretical output levels represents a waste that can be slowly eliminated through process innovations and improved procedures. Theoretical capacity measures can be developed and do work.

Unfortunately, most companies do not start from the "best we can be" in defining their baseline capacity. Instead, companies use a broad range of measures, including *practical capacity* (theoretical capacity adjusted for "normal" downtime and waste), *normal capacity* (the average output of the plant, in terms of either earned hours or units produced, over a period of three to five years), *budgeted or planned* capacity (the current year's projected output volumes), and finally *actual capacity* (the actual output volumes for the reporting period).

As the diagram shows, as the defined or expected capacity levels are dropped, waste soars. The problem is that it is hidden waste—hidden in the measurement process before anyone is really aware of the cost and implications of idled resources.

Back-Office Capacities

A nonmanufacturing or back-office operation that moves paper or transactions instead of physical materials has a defined capacity. While a bit harder to measure than the capacity of a JIT cell or a plant, the service capability of an organization is as essential to its long-term success as its physical capacity. Many companies, in fact, consist solely of invisible flows of transactions with little or no visible trace of the value being created. Yet each of these systems or processes has a defined ability to do work—a capacity. Few companies attempt to measure this type of capacity, which is unfortunate because it costs just as much to purchase and use as physical capacity in a manufacturing plant.

Stratus Computer's push to contain costs in the back office through budgeting represents one way a company can gauge potential capacity. Do people currently work flat out every minute they're in the office? Of those hours, how many are really productive? Are good people being asked to do less than good things, resulting in excess waste and cost? Where does the workflow seem to be hung up (where is the bottleneck)? In developing answers to these questions, a company can begin to understand its back-office capacity. These questions need to be asked *before* any additional resources are added to the office.

Another way to gauge the potential capacity of the back office is to follow an order from the time it is received until the requested product or service is delivered to the customer. This is an enlightening, and perhaps frightening, exercise in most companies. At a medium-sized manufacturing company in Pennsylvania, a process map of the paperwork flow was developed as part of a study to determine why materials weren't reaching the plant floor on time.

When the map was laid out in all of its detail, the paperwork flow was a nightmare. Customers were being promised two-week delivery times when it took almost a week to get the order past all the managers who wanted to "know" it was in-house (and affix their signature of approval to it).

By the time purchasing received a request for materials, the order was already late. Yet before the process mapping was done, the finger of blame for late deliveries was being pointed at purchasing. How could purchasing obtain the material on time? There was so much waste built into the paperwork flow that it prevented the company from meeting customer expectations. Today, more and more companies are realizing that paperwork-handling procedures—developed piecemeal over time and never reexamined for logic, effectiveness, or efficiency—are the real bottlenecks in the company. Back-office capacity is being devoured by ineffectiveness or structural waste.

Building Waste into a System

There are many ways that waste is built into capacity measurement and management. First, the way a system, process, or product line is structured can build in waste. Defined around the bottleneck resource, this form of capacity-based waste is caused by how the work is defined and routed and not by how much of it is done. The flip side of *structural waste* is the failure to use all the available capacity of the bottleneck resource. The term used to describe underutilization of available capacity is *idle capacity*. Capacity can be idled for a broad number of reasons, including insufficient sales volumes, excess capability in total, and poorly defined management policies. In addition, the definition of baseline capacity, as well as the standard cost estimates used to charge capacity costs to product, can create hidden layers of waste that are hard to see and even harder to eliminate.

Structural waste is actually caused by an accounting fact of life called the *behavior of costs*. What does this mean? When all the technical jargon is pushed aside, this concept reduces to a simple fact: you can't buy resources in exactly the amount needed. The size of the resource's *purchase package*, its *divisibility* (how easily it can be parceled out in smaller units as needed), and its *storability* combine to put boundaries around the amount of resource capacity that can actually be used before the resource loses value. These characteristics of an input, and how easily it can be traced to a unit of output, result in the designation of a cost as fixed, variable, semifixed, or semivariable. Understanding these cost behaviors is an essential part of identifying and managing structural waste.

The effect of "lumpy" resources on a company's total costs and total structural waste is significant (see Figure 6.2). For every "lumpy" (fixed or semifixed) cost, there is a large potential for wasted capacity. It is difficult to match the total amount of the asset's capacity to the amount of work it will be required to support. Unless the capacity of the resource can be stored, this mismatch between a resource's potential to create value and the amount of it that can be used, *given the structure and volume of work performed,* results in waste.

Equally important is the effect of "lumpy" resources on a system's performance. It is easy to talk about "balancing" a workflow through a system, but the reality is that the bottleneck resource prevents the full use—ever—of many of the company's fixed and semifixed resources. This is the essence of structural waste: the capacity of some resources will always be thrown away simply because this resource is constrained within a system that has less effective capacity, in total, than the resource has alone. If a machine's capacity is 10,000 units per hour, but it feeds a machine that has a top speed of 5,000 units per hour, 50 percent of the potential capacity of the first machine will be permanently idled.

Measurements can be developed to track structural waste in a system, as suggested by Table 6.1. A "waste meter" can be used to identify how much of each resource within a system can really be used given the capacity of the bottleneck resource. This embedded waste, seldom considered or measured, represents a permanent loss of potential profits. It is a waste that cannot be recouped, recycled, or

FIGURE 6.2 LUMPY RESOURCES AND WASTE

Minimizing waste begins with understanding a company's "behavior of costs"

Resource 1: Machine

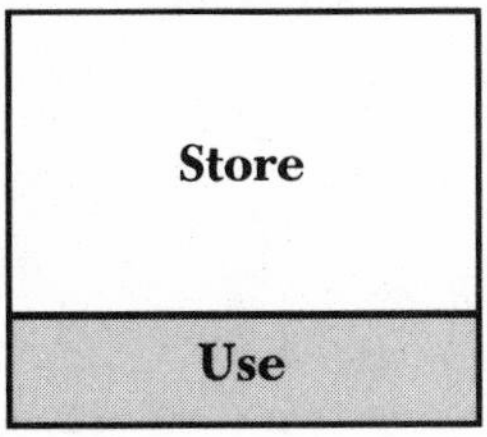

Store
Use

If you can store the unused value of a resource, it doesn't matter how big a purchase package it comes in: waste will be minimized over time.

Resource 2: Labor

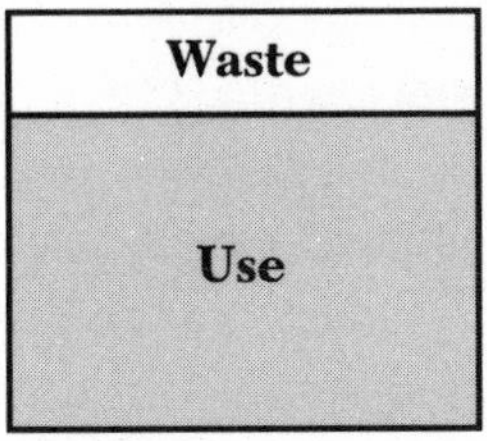

Waste
Use

If a resource is bought in fairly small purchase packages—*it is semivariable*—whatever isn't used will be wasted, but this can be minimized.

Resource 3: Rented copier

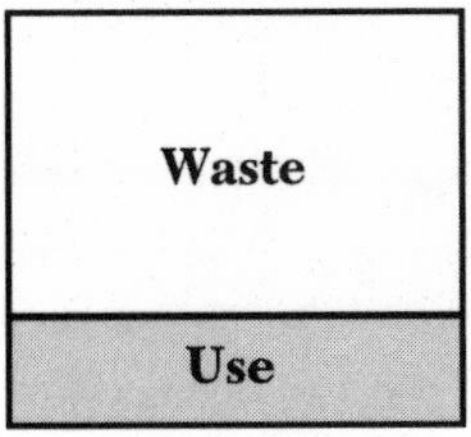

Waste
Use

If a resource has to be bought in fairly large purchase packages—it is *semifixed*—the level of potential waste will be very high.

121

TABLE 6.1 WASTE EMBEDDED IN SYSTEMS: ORDER-TAKING ACTIVITY

Resource	Total capacity	Used capacity	Waste	Waste meter
Clerks	24,000 orders	18,000 orders	25%	
Telephone: Basic	8,640 hours per line; 3 lines per dept.	2,000 hours per line	77%	
Telephone: Long-distance charge	Bought by minute	100%	0%	
Desks	Indefinite	2,000 hours each	?	
Computer	8,640 hours per computer; 4 in department	2,000 hours each	77%	
Space charges	8,640 hours per year	2,000 hours per year	77%	
Manager	2,000 hours per year	2,000 hours per year	0%[a]	
Supplies	Bought as needed	100%	0%	
Training, taxes, insurance	Bought as needed	100%	0%[b]	

a. Knowing the manager is "busy" supervising people for the entire number of hours that he or she works isn't the same as saying that everything the manager does is value creating. This is one resource we could look into further to see exactly what is done for the 2,000 hours, why, and if better use could be made of the resource.

b. Training is a resource that actually has a long life: it lasts for the entire time an employee works for a firm. Companies are beginning to treat training as an investment in future value-creation ability, but it remains difficult to assign a capacity and useful life to this item.

reclaimed. The only way to minimize this waste is to recognize it and then seek ways to either better use the wasted capacity of these resources or to increase the capacity of the system. Since you have to buy the resource in the preset purchase package, there are few options left for dealing with this "excess."

In addition to developing the waste meter and better understanding how much profit potential is being thrown away, it is often useful to load the fully constrained cost of a system on its bottleneck. Goldratt and Cox make this suggestion in *The Goal*, noting that when a bottleneck machine is idle or inefficiently used, the actual cost to the company isn't $20 per hour but rather $2,735.[1] Goldratt and Cox recount a conversation between Jonah and Lou, the plant accountant, that illustrates the issues surrounding structural waste and its impact on profitability:

> *"What you have learned is that the capacity of the plant is equal to the capacity of its bottlenecks," says Jonah. "Whatever the bottlenecks produce in an hour is the equivalent of what the plant produces in an hour. So . . . an hour lost at a bottleneck is an hour lost for the entire system."*
>
> *"Right, we're with you," says Lou.*
>
> *"Then how much would it cost for this entire plant to be idle for one hour?" asks Jonah.*
>
> *"I really can't say, but it would be very expensive," admits Lou.*
>
> *"The actual cost of the bottleneck is the total expense of the system divided by the number of hours the bottleneck produces," says Jonah.*

While much more dialogue takes place around the concept of a system's capacity and the bottleneck resource, the message in this brief exchange is clear: a system is constrained by a bottleneck. The cost of this constraint is a function of the amount of structural waste— waste of other resources tied to the bottleneck—that is built into the system, process, or workflow *when it is designed*. It is a waste that needs to be measured when the system is built, again when changes are made to the workflow, assets, or processes that are embedded in the system, and finally on an ongoing basis as the cost of idle capacity.

"USE IT OR LOSE IT": IDLE CAPACITY AND WASTE

Waste is worse than loss. The time is coming when every person who lays claim to ability will keep the question of waste before him constantly. The scope of thrift is limitless.

THOMAS A. EDISON (4)

Idle capacity is the result of poor use of a system's potential to create value. It has many causes, including

- The baseline definition of capacity used,

- Management of the system and process flows,

- Shortfalls in market demand, mix changes, and related marketing-based issues,

- Accounting approaches, such as standard costing, and

- Unplanned interruptions to the workflow.

Each of these root causes of idle capacity creates a unique and measurable level of waste. Unless the assets that make up the system's capacity can be stored, this loss is immediate and irreversible. Waste created by idle capacity should and can be measured on an ongoing basis within the confines of any accounting- or operational-based performance evaluation system. Obtaining the measurement starts with understanding the causes of the cost.

Flawed Measurements and Idle Capacity

Two causes of idle capacity–based waste are linked to the measurement methods used by many companies. The baseline definition of capacity, discussed earlier, can now be expanded to include the effects of structural waste. When a company adds resources to any system, it creates the potential for structural waste. If the added resources aren't focused on increasing the capacity of the bottleneck, this increase in waste is guaranteed.

If you think about the levels of structural waste built into a system at its design, and add the use of flawed baseline measures of the capacity of the bottleneck, the scope of the problem becomes clearer. Permanently idle capacity is created by using baseline measures that assume inefficiency and waste will be present. And as the amount of resources dedicated to the system grows, so does the level of waste assumed into the baseline capacity measure. The result is a "ratchet effect": waste grows not only in absolute terms but also as a percentage of the total resources used by a firm (see Figure 6.3).

Using flawed measurements of baseline capacity permanently idles the resources dedicated to a process—not because of the bottleneck but because of the assumptions that govern the use of the bottleneck resource. In a world driven by measurements and a "meet standard" mentality, setting baseline capacity measures that accept a loss of 15 to 20 percent of the potential profits from a process is hardly logical. But that is exactly what a company does when it uses normal rather than theoretical capacity as its basis for evaluating the performance of a cell, process, or system.

One major form of resistance to using theoretical capacity measures is the ongoing belief that they (1) are impossible to measure and (2) demotivate people because perfection can never be reached. The first point is well taken, but several suggestions have been made in this chapter for how to estimate the potential capacity of a bottleneck (which is easier to assess than systemic capacity). While the measure may not be perfect, it will create the right type of behavior. This leads to the second point—the motivational effect of theoretical capacity measures.

The key driver of behavior is not the measurement itself but *how that measurement is used.* If people are punished for failing to meet the theoretical standard, they will be demotivated. The theoretical standard can never be reached: it's a theoretical standard and is reachable only in theory. Does that make it useless or even harmful? Not really, in fact, a theoretical standard can motivate people to try

FIGURE 6.3 WASTED CAPACITY: A RATCHET EFFECT

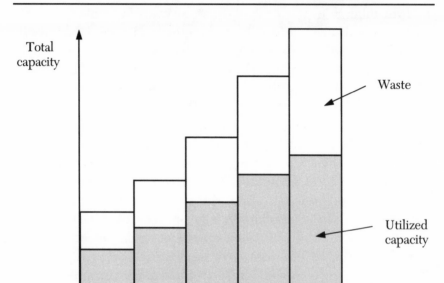

harder than ever before because it creates an environment of challenge. Most people love a challenge if they feel they will be rewarded for trying. Winning does not mean meeting the theoretical level of performance; it means improving and moving toward perfection. The fun is in the trying, as long as no one punishes you for taking the risk in the first place.

Standard Costs and Waste

Standard costing is the most frequently used form of accounting in the Western world. A standard cost model focuses on developing an estimate of the resources needed to produce one unit of output (a good or service). What often is not realized is that a level of waste is built into these measures, and once buried in the measurement, the assumed waste never disappears.

What types of waste are assumed into a standard cost?

- The baseline measure of the potential output of a person or machine is defined according to practical capacity. Definitional waste is once again an issue because of this practice.

- The measure assumes that a prespecified level of downtime, scrap, and "normal" levels of waste will take place. Since it's going to happen anyway, it's built into the standard.

- The focus of the standard is on one machine or one person—not on the system. So all the issues surrounding structural waste are encapsulated in the standard cost estimate.

- The measurement developed is efficiency driven. The goal it promotes is keeping everyone busy, whether the work being done is value adding or waste.

- Standard cost estimates promote the "meet standard" mentality. People are rewarded for meeting the preset standard and wasting exactly the right amount of time and resources. If too few resources are wasted, a "favorable" variance is created; if too many resources are used, an "unfavorable" variance is generated.

The standard cost measure rarely focuses on the best use of resources for the company as a whole—it concentratess on one machine or one person. That means that a logical decision to offload work from the bottleneck to a slower machine or process will create an unfavorable efficiency variance *even though the company is reducing waste* by using more of its capacity, generating more revenue by finishing more work, and in all likelihood improving its performance against customer expectations. It makes more sense to use a less efficient process if the result is an improvement in total use of system capacity, but the standard cost measure will signal that a mistake has taken place. This particular idiosyncrasy of the standard costing model is the reason that experts such as Eli Goldratt advocate eliminating it. The measures create behavior that increases the waste and decreases the potential profits created by the firm.

The paradoxes of the standard costing model, unfortunately, go even a bit deeper. Variances are created every period without fail, pushed through the budgeting games (such as pass the variance, flavor of the month, and so on), and then dumped into the general ledger to balance the books (see Figure 6.4). Is the variance analyzed to determine whether performance over the long term is improving? No. Is the variance used to update the standard, making the estimate a more accurate picture of actual performance? No. In fact, the variance can't be used for updating standards in most cases because the standard is built from engineering estimates and models, and the variance is developed in the accounting system. Seldom, if ever, will these two systems of measurement agree.

This leaves the million-dollar question: What does happen to the variance? It is dumped into the garbage can—the general ledger used by accountants to keep the basic equation "Assets equal Liabilities plus Owner's Equity" in balance. The variance is used to generate an accounting transaction to balance the books. That is all it is used for. Many feel that is all it is good for. Whatever a person's level of comfort with and appreciation for the accounting system, it is hard to believe that this is the best use of this potentially valuable measurement (it is a gap measure, after all).

What can be done about this seemingly illogical state of affairs? Two changes would fix the problem: (1) substitute average historical costs for the engineered cost estimate and (2) trend the average cost against the theoretical baseline measure to encourage continuous improvement. The first suggestion runs counter to what many accountants learn in school: traditional accounting textbooks dismiss historical standards *because they are felt to build in an acceptance of current levels of waste.* In other words, if it currently costs $3.00 to process a monthly checking account statement, we don't know if $2.50 is the "right" cost if everything goes as planned—fifty cents of waste gets built in to the "standard."

FIGURE 6.4 DUMPING THE VARIANCES

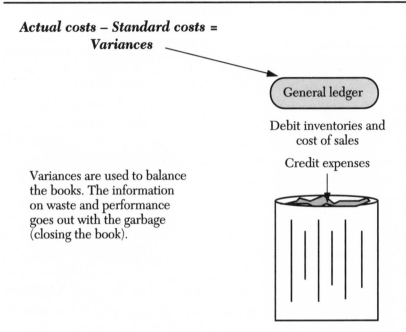

Actual costs – Standard costs =
Variances

General ledger

Debit inventories and
cost of sales

Credit expenses

Variances are used to balance
the books. The information
on waste and performance
goes out with the garbage
(closing the book).

Interesting. Engineered standards, by design, build waste into their estimates of potential performance and resource use. Yet this type of built-in waste is overlooked, while measurement of the waste embedded in current practices is rejected. Building in waste is not acceptable, but a measurement that hides the truth about how much waste is really present in a system is *not* better than one that spells it out. The key to the usefulness of either measurement approach is the baseline measure of capacity. Theoretical capacity, not practical, normal, or actual utilization, is the soundest basis for action.

The second point returns our focus to the way a measurement is used. If a rolling average of historical actual costs is compared against the theoretical standard, an objective evaluation of current performance and the degree of improvement can be taken. In addition, if the variance created by the difference between historical actual costs and current performance is used to update the standard, the trending of the standard over time can be used as a measure of continuous improvement.

Many companies that have successfully implemented just-in-time manufacturing have moved to using a rolling average of historical actual costs as a main measure of cell performance. This number is trended over time, and negative patterns (such as increased average costs) are the basis for new improvement efforts. Motorola, AT&T, Stanadyne Diesel Company, Hewlett-Packard, and Texas Instruments have found that actual cost-based standards, used appropriately, are one of the best tools available to monitor and motivate performance.

Once the measure is made objective, honest, and accurate, it can be used to create positive behavior that results in increased profits and decreased waste. Burying this information, and the knowledge it contains, in the general ledger may be one of the worst forms of waste detailed in this book because it deflates expectations and creates a game when action is what really is needed.

Managing a System to Minimize Waste

Systemic management includes the ongoing elements of balancing a line and encouraging effective, efficient use of all resources, the assumptions made about the "best" way to direct these efforts, and the way in which interruptions to the workflow are generated and handled. Assumptions about the balancing and use of a system or process are the essence of how management decides what to do and when, and where to do it.

Even when capacity is defined based on a bottleneck, current management practices are usually taken as a given. At a medium-sized bicycle manufacturer in the Midwest, for example, the paint booth was identified as the limiting factor of production. Management recognized this fact and believed that the paint booth was being operated "at capacity." That meant the plant's ability to create value was limited: there was no slack left to make more product.

The problem facing the company was that demand for the company's products exceeded the assumed capacity of the paint booth, but environmental protection laws made it impossible to add more painting capacity. When queried about the assumptions surrounding the paint booth's use, management revealed that "full" use of this resource did not include a third shift or work on the weekends. Since the company could sell every bicycle it could make, this waste of potential capacity—based on existing management practices surrounding the number of shifts and days worked—was avoidable. Management practices and assumptions, not the bottleneck resource, were limiting output.

At Bradford Soap Works, management practices are creating idle capacity in the way that work is bundled. In this plant, packaging machines are normally attached to the end of a soap line based on the type of packaging required by the customer. Since Bradford is a job shop, though, these packaging requirements are constantly changing. The result is packaging machines on wheels, being rolled into a line based on customer requirements.

Placing the packaging machines on wheels seems like a logical way to deal with the high level of variety the company experiences in meeting customer needs, but in reality the tradeoff being made is between two-stage production and structural idle capacity: both increase the total costs of doing business. First, the packaging machines run slower than the press that turns out the bars of soap. The press is slowed down, and any excess production over the capacity of the packaging machines is "re"worked or wasted. First-pass yields on these integrated lines can be quite low at times. A second problem that emerges is that the packaging machines are difficult to set up and synchronize. The result is high levels of interruptions or unplanned downtime due to packaging machine malfunctions after the soap run is under way.

A third problem caused by bundling packaging tightly to the

soap-making process is high setup times due to a myriad of problems emerging from moving these sensitive machines around and trying to balance the processing speeds of multiple machines. In total, then, the management policy to bundle two very different processes together creates high levels of idle capacity and waste of press ability, low first-pass yields, high levels of interruptions, and high idle time for setups. If these costs could be compared to the cost of hiring a person to offload the soap bars into a kanban tray for movement to one of several preset packaging configurations, a sound decision could be made about when to bundle machines and when to separate them. Unfortunately, this information isn't collected at the company, and so the waste continues.

Interruptions and Other Maladies

Management affects capacity use and waste in many different ways. While the basic assumptions governing the process create one form of waste, the way a company responds to customer requests, maintenance needs, and other forms of potential and actual interruptions to the workflow create their own unique layers of waste.

The group of people most responsible for interrupting work on the plant floor is management. "Hot" orders don't magically appear one day; someone has to make them "hot." A machine operator doesn't have this authority: management does. Hot orders, pushed through the production process, trigger rework, more setups, more confusion, more handling, and more waste than almost any other single activity performed in a company. The irony is that in attempting to respond to a customer request or to put out a fire, others are lit. Logically, if the workflow has been planned to maximize on-time delivery, any delay that pops up will quite likely result in late deliveries. That means more "hot" orders, more interruptions, and more "re's" throughout the back office and plant floor.

Soon everything going through the plant is "hot." Paperwork is in a shambles as product starts shipping before materials can even be formally received into the inventory system. Ongoing work orders are interrupted and often are set aside or even lost, resulting in endless rounds of hide-and-seek to uncover the misplaced materials and products. And so the waste proliferates—created by good intentions and implemented with poor methods.

Interruptions also can be created by unplanned machine breakdowns, material shortages, poor-quality parts, and poorly controlled workflows. Interruptions to a workflow create waste. Eliminating the waste is as simple as finding a way to eliminate the interruption, whether by creating a "hot" shop with prototyping capability (to minimize these interruptions and excess capacity losses in the hot shop), developing better materials control procedures, or implementing a total preventive maintenance (TPM) system.

The best solution of all, of course, is to manage the plant so that interruptions simply don't occur because the plant is flexible, parts are available, and product ships on time. Building inventory is not a solution, unless the waste it creates is the least costly alternative the company has at its command. Since this will seldom be the case, the solution lies in preventing interruptions by managing processes better. If management is the prime source of interruptions, then, like Pogo, they have to recognize that they have seen the enemy, and it is us. No one can stop this type of waste except the people who create it.

A Basic Model for Measuring Capacity-Based Waste

The measurement of capacity-based waste breaks down into two basic pieces: (1) determining how much capacity is currently being wasted and (2) identifying the causes for the waste. The first part of this measurement problem is fairly straightforward:

$$\text{Idle capacity} = \text{Theoretical capacity} - \text{Actual capacity}$$

$$\text{Cost of Idleness} = \text{Idle capacity} \times \text{Target profit per unit}$$

These are the only numbers needed to grasp the full effect of idle capacity on plant or company profitability. They are simple measures and easily calculated, graphed, and analyzed. When combined with the development of continuous improvement-based standards, trended over time (as well as a full understanding of the structural waste embedded in the value-creation system) these measures provide all the basic information needed to focus attention on maximizing capacity use.

The second capacity-measurement issue requires a method for classifying the causes for the idle capacity and attempting to assign some estimate of the total waste created by each cause. One way to accomplish this is to create a cause-and-effect diagram (see Figure 6.5) reminiscent of the Ishikawa fishbone diagram. As is typical of these types of diagrams, the goal is to analyze the varied causes of capacity-based waste and then identify the causes that are most significant.

A second approach that can be used for measuring actual capacity utilization and the causes of idleness is to create a twenty-four-hour machine utilization report for each process or machining center (see

FIGURE 6.5 DIAGNOSING IDLE CAPACITY AND ITS CAUSES

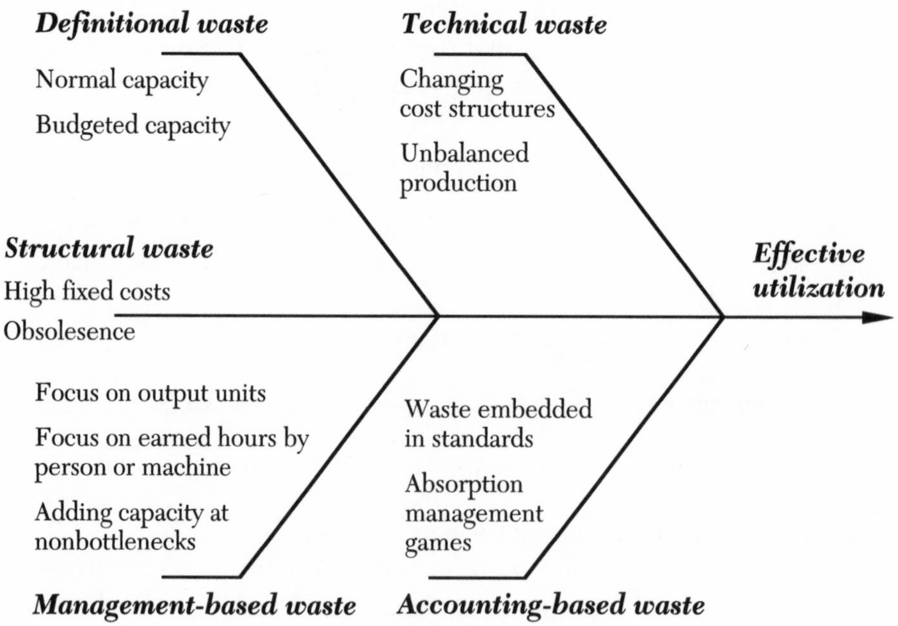

Definitional waste

Normal capacity

Budgeted capacity

Technical waste

Changing cost structures

Unbalanced production

Structural waste

High fixed costs

Obsolesence

Effective utilization

Focus on output units

Focus on earned hours by person or machine

Adding capacity at nonbottlenecks

Waste embedded in standards

Absorption management games

Management-based waste   *Accounting-based waste*

Figure 6.6). The advantage of this report is that it can combine several different reporting functions in one, such as machine reliabilities, setup times and cost, material shortages, and productive time per order. This report can be tailored to pick up all relevant shop floor information—by machine, machine center, or cell—in one easily completed form. Finally, an exception reporting system could be developed to track the causes of interruptions on the plant floor and in the back office. Whichever method is used, the goal is clear: eliminating waste starts with making it visible.

Market Shortfalls and Other Woes

One final potential cause of idle capacity is market shortfalls. These can be due to a wide variety of "misses," such as inaccurate forecasts, shifts in customer demand, macroeconomic effects, a poor fit between the product and customer expectations, competitive pressures, mix changes, oversupply, seasonality, and misinformation. Whatever the cause, the result is excess capacity and increased waste.

This type of idle capacity is, theoretically, the easiest to address: sell more product! But in the competitive global marketplace this may not always be possible. There may be more producers of a service or product than there are customers, less money available for spending, shifts in consumer demand, and so on. If the excess capacity appears to be permanent, it has to be redeployed or eliminated. Otherwise it will form a permanent drag on the company's profits. Flexible excess capacity is far less of a problem than inflexible machines and processes. If the machine or process can be easily redeployed to do other work, then the impact of marketing shifts on company profits can be minimized. The goal is to improve the responsiveness and flexibility of the production process while reducing the company's exposure to changes in the market.

The role of flexibility in reducing idle-capacity costs has not always been understood. For many years the driving force behind finding volume to fill up idle machines has been the mantra, "Spread fixed costs out over more units." What does this mean? In many companies,

FIGURE 6.6 TRACKING CAPACITY UTILIZATION

Date __8/15/94__   Line/Machine #: __602__

Job #	Start time	Stop time	Reason	Action
G4153	8⁰⁰ AM	8⁴⁵	Set up	
	8⁴⁵	10³⁰	Run 'til hit defects	Recalibrate ?
	10³⁰	10⁴⁵		Recalibrate & check
	10⁴⁵	12⁰⁰	Run 'til lunch break	
	12⁰⁰	12³⁰	Lunch	
	12³⁰	1⁴⁵	Stop due to material shortage	Stop job; 15,000 done 5,000 short
G5232	1⁴⁵	3⁰⁰	Set up	

the volume of work across the machine, and its relationship to the average fixed cost of production that needs to be charged to every unit produced to cover these fixed charges, has been the key measure of concern. Reported as a *volume variance*, any misses between planned production levels and actual levels have been filtered through to the inventoried cost of a good unit.

A volume variance is a poor proxy for an idle capacity charge. A volume variance does not really spell out how much capacity is idle and where; it focuses on the difference between budgeted and actual production levels. Recalling the earlier discussion of definitional capacity waste, the weakness of the volume variance is easy to see: it doesn't report waste; it hides it by spreading it out over actual production. In addition, because the volume variance is reported at the plant level rather than companywide, it becomes too easy to assign responsibility for this variance to manufacturing.

Manufacturing can control only its own behavior. It has little or no direct influence on customer demand in the short term, although it can affect it in the long term through quality, cost, delivery, and responsiveness. Both marketing and management have to bear responsibility for filling the machines or office with work. The people doing the work can't find work. When they do, it is often "make-work" to increase their earned or worked hours. Since the profitability of the company depends on making only what is needed when it is needed, any form of make-work is to be avoided. It is waste dressed up as productivity. Make-work—or producing to work-in-process inventory or other related irrelevancies—lulls everyone into believing that money is being made when in fact it is being thrown away.

Price cuts are one strategy companies have traditionally used to increase the volume of business through a plant or office. Cutting prices, though, is dangerous unless the company knows it can survive long-term if it continues selling its products at a reduced price. If a company is pricing at market and constantly pushing its costs down to stay within this market envelope, it will be better able to respond to market pressures with decisions that make sense in the long term.

Target costing follows a simple logic: price down, cost down. This is a sustainable strategy; indiscriminate price cutting is not.

One final point needs to be discussed—the difference between effective and efficient capacity utilization. One of the biggest dangers faced by a company that develops capacity measurements is that they can drive employees to produce goods and services whether or not there is a market for them. While inadequate demand is one cause of idle capacity, filling up capacity to make products for which there is no demand is not a solution for either a marketing problem or a utilization shortfall. In fact, this type of response to idle the capacity concerns creates more waste than it eliminates, unless the company knows with certainty that the product will be needed and soon. Swapping one form of waste for another is not forward movement; it is a counterproductive game.

Any company faced with permanent excess capacity must eliminate it. Hiding the waste by spreading it out over actual production can put the company into a death spiral, as costs per unit produced soar and profits plummet. The shortfalls between theoretical capacity and actual capacity use have to be identified, analyzed, and managed for elimination if a long-term, sustainable competitive position is to be attained. Failing to plan capacity to match projected market volumes, to match specific capacity to process and product characteristics, and to employ flexible machines and methods wherever possible will result in idle capacity and reduced profits. The only question that remains is when will it occur, not if.

IDLE CAPACITY AND IDLE MINDS

"Just take a look behind you," says Jonah. "Take a look at the monster you've made. It did not create itself. You have created this mountain of inventory with your own decisions. And why? Because of the wrong assumptions that you must make the workers produce one hundred percent of the time, or else get rid of them."

GOLDRATT AND COX
The Goal, p. 208

Mountains of inventory have often been seen as a better "waste" of company resources than idle people. This management belief can be traced to several factors:

- The perceived high cost of idle people,

- The tendency to value brawn over brains in the labor force,

- Poor understanding of the underlying waste created by make-work, and

- The perceived nonstorability of labor-based costs.

Since the third factor has been discussed above, misperceptions and the myths surrounding the role of labor in value creation are addressed here.

What's in a Cost?

In the early years of the industrial revolution, the costs of production were distributed in the following way: materials, 50 percent; labor, 40 percent; and overhead and other charges, 10 percent. People were a significant cost element in this setting, and keeping people busy made sense. They were the core factor of productivity and the defining element of capacity. Almost the only control a company had over its cost structure in this setting was control over the amount of labor used to produce its products and provide its services.

If the same analysis is made of a manufacturing company today, the distribution of costs is this: materials, 50 percent; labor, 5 percent; and overhead, 45 percent. If the company provides services instead of physical goods, the distribution is something like this: labor, 40 percent; and overhead, 60 percent. While the figures can be debated (maybe labor is 1 percent in one company and 25 percent in another), the trend is clear: direct labor as a percentage of total cost in any type of a company is decreasing. It appears that machines have replaced humans.

This being the case, why has management, which never should be assumed to be ignorant or slow to catch on to trends, persisted in focusing on labor? First, there is a tendency to want people to work for their money. The Puritan work ethic is still with us, driving us to work and to keep those around us busy. Yet one would be hard pressed to accept this explanation as the sole reason for the continued focus on direct labor "idleness."

Pushing below the surface, a more viable explanation emerges for the continued focus on keeping labor busy. In most companies today, overhead (the 45 percent) is charged out on direct labor hours or dollars. If a direct laborer works, she pulls with her a major chunk of overhead; if she doesn't work, this overhead remains unassigned to "output." Unassigned overhead results in a volume variance. And so the game continues. The volume variance, or the way accounting treats overhead expense, appears to create a mentality of waste in terms of unnecessary work. This work is done to absorb cost that is not caused by people: it is caused by machines, methods, and support activities. Since this cost is attached to people, though, the cost of an idle person becomes not only the wage being paid but the *wage plus overhead.*

To illustrate the point, let's assume that the 50-5-45 percent distribution of costs translates to how one dollar of cost is spent in a company to make one unit of output. In other words, the product cost will consist of fifty cents material, five cents labor, and forty-five cents overhead. For every penny spent on labor, ten cents will be charged to the product—one cent of labor and nine cents of overhead. Clearly, then, if the one cent of labor is translated to ten cents of chargeable cost, it becomes more important in everyone's mind to keep labor busy absorbing overhead through production.

While this may look like a strange way to deal with the costs of overhead and its effect on profitability, it is, unfortunately, the most common approach being taken in companies today. It drives companies to replace people with machines, which drives up the overhead percentage of the total product cost even more, resulting in higher labor-based overhead rates, leading to even more labor cuts. This vicious cycle undermines the flexibility and long-term survival of the organization as its human capital is eroded.

Recasting the Problem: Labor as Capital, Capital as Waste

The underlying message in the above example is that labor is an asset that has long-term value. It is not, except in very rare cases, the primary driver of cost. In fact, the best use a company can make of its "idle" labor time is training. Training increases the value of the human capital in a company, increases its flexibility, and decreases its overall waste. Well-trained people can step into the breach created by market shifts, machine problems, or changing technology to allow the company to continue turning out high-quality product on time. Labor is the most flexible resource a company has. And whether paid on an hourly or a monthly basis, labor is a semivariable cost of production. That means, quite simply, that any excess labor capacity can be adjusted much more easily than excess machines.

Well-trained labor can help management redesign a workflow, identify sources of quality and throughput problems, discover process and product improvements, and build a solid reputation and market for the company's outputs. Companies like Hewlett-Packard, Texas Instruments, Motorola, Xerox, and others have shifted their perspective on labor, treating it as a resource, not a liability. At Hewlett-Packard, direct labor is placed into the overhead pool rather than the other way around. This change has reduced the number of accounting transactions that are triggered during the production process, while focusing everyone's attention on the core issue: making good product that meets customer expectations. Using flexible, people-intensive, just-in-time production cells, Hewlett-Packard is able to absorb rapid production shifts in volume and models produced.

In this new system, materials receive much more of management's attention at Hewlett-Packard. Recognizing that materials and activities are primary cost drivers, the company focuses on establishing baseline estimates of the cost of these elements. The result has been increased use of standard parts, decreasing inventories, increased design for manufacturability, and a sustainable competitive position. Using labor as a resource, as both a brain as well as muscle, Hewlett-Packard has found a way to thrive in the fiercely competitive electronics market. An idle person at Hewlett-Packard is either redirected to maintenance, cleaning, training, problem solving, process redesign, quality improvement or sent home with pay. No one is simply kept busy: this facade of productivity has been uncovered for the waste that it is.

Numbers, Mindsets, and Idle Capacity

In the final analysis, the key to sustainable growth is to have the right mix of people and machines focused on producing what the customer requires, when it is needed. Machines are not to be preferred over people or people over machines. Instead, the goal is to find the combination of resources that provides for efficiency and flexibility in the value-creation process. Machines may seem more efficient in terms of how fast they can make a unit or perform an operation, but this speed is valuable only if it can be fully used. Idle resources are waste unless they can be easily redeployed to other ongoing work or to developing the capability for doing work in the future.

Measuring and tracking structural capacity waste, idle capacity, and the effective use of human resources are at the heart of the profit potential for every company, no matter what its size or what type of work it does. People, long perceived to be the "enemy" in the profitability game, are increasingly being seen as the best asset a company can buy. Relatively inexpensive, flexible, trainable, and purchased in small "packages" of capability, people represent a viable solution to the high-technology, high-fixed-cost world of automation.

Changing mindsets, changing numbers, and ensuring that a company's fixed assets are actively deployed to value-creating work are the only sustainable paths forward for any organization. By measuring and reporting capacity-based waste, accurately and objectively, a company can focus its attention on balance and flexibility rather than make-work. The choice is between sustainable growth and the death spiral: there are few other options in a global marketplace.

There are risks and costs to a program of action. But they are far less than the long-range risks and costs of comfortable inaction.
JOHN F. KENNEDY (1)

CHAPTER 7

Assets That Aren't and Other Conundrums

Try and find your deepest issue in every confusion, and abide by that.

D. H. LAWRENCE
Selected Essays (1)

Words bring with them a meaning that drives action and thought. In the business world, words such as *profit* create images of growth and health, while the term *loss* drives everyone to update their resumés in preparation for cost-reduction programs. The value of a firm is defined in accounting terms such as *assets, net worth,* and *liabilities.* The results of a company's daily operations are summarized in terms of *revenues* and *expenses, standards* and *variances, cost of goods sold,* and the bottom line—*net income.* Each of these terms conjures up a view of the organization and its ability to create value for its customers. They are all part of the language of business— *accounting.*

Using accounting language to describe the activities that take place in a company is logical. The world of debits and credits, assets and liabilities, and owner's equity is a stable one where rules and regulations curb the use of "creative" numbers and objectivity rules the day. Accounting serves as a language because it can be relied on to mean something specific, each and every time it is used. By providing society with a basic shorthand for describing business events, accounting serves many users and many uses.

Despite its advantages, however, this language and its behavioral effect on the firm is not all positive. What do people do when faced with a negative variance? If something is called an asset, how do people use it and view it? Is a resource any less valuable because the accounting system books it as an expense rather than an asset? Clearly, making a judgment about a resource's value-creating potential on the basis of the noun used to describe it (such as *expense* versus *asset*) leaves open the potential for error. To avoid these and related errors, management has to step away from the language of accounting and examine accounting's effect on everyday life in the organization.

INVENTORY: ASSET OR LIABILITY?

Success doesn't come from the way you think it does, it comes from the way you think.

ROBERT SCHULLER (6)

Inventory is one of the major short-term assets held by most companies. Consisting of raw materials, work-in-process, and finished goods, inventory is the engine that drives the value-creation process. Without materials, product can't be made. On the other hand, excessive inventory levels generate new forms of waste on almost a daily basis. The goal is to find a balance point between too little inventory and too much. The answer, though, may not lie in buffer stocks and economic order quantity (EOQ) models, but rather in flexibility and a balancing of the various types of waste inventory creates.

As the Inventory Turns . . .

One of the most common measures used to evaluate the effectiveness
of a company's inventory-handling procedures is inventory turns.
Inventory turns are defined as follows:

$$\frac{\text{Inventory}}{\text{turns}} = \frac{\text{Cost of goods sold}}{\text{Average inventory value}}$$

This ratio provides a global assessment of the number of times a
company "uses up" its inventory in the course of a year. Inventory turns
are often seen as one barometer of management effectiveness: more
turns mean better management. Yet the number doesn't indicate what
part of the inventory is turning, nor does it prevent the recurrence of
major inventory writedowns due to obsolescence, writedowns, "es-
capes" (shortages), and damage (OWED). OWED, or the waste from
ineffective inventory management, is a constant reminder of how a
company can throw away its profits. Controlling inventory and measuring how many times it turns in a year are two very different things.

Controlling inventory means knowing what you've got, where it is,
when it will be needed, and what the optimal "shelf life" is for its
various components. In addition, controlling inventory means managing it wisely; running out of the nuts and bolts needed to produce a
car is not a good idea. This fact has led many companies to developing
an A-B-C approach to inventory management. The basic idea is that A
items, which have a significant cost element, are tightly controlled.
Damage, obsolescence, or shortages of these items are expensive
propositions. B items, on the other hand, are major parts that may
have a long lead time or have some other defining characteristic that
makes it important to balance the amount ordered and held versus the
cost and risk of obtaining it at all. Finally, C items are the nuts and
bolts of organizational life. Missing due dates because of a shortage of
C items is not acceptable to anyone.

What is waste in terms of inventory management, then? Having too many A items or too few C's is one way waste can be gauged. A second type of waste is excessive time and effort spent managing C items: they should be treated as no-brainers. Simply keep enough on hand, and make sure you never run out. In fact, while the cost to hold A items is the largest, the waste created by running out of C items is higher.

The reason for this apparent contradiction is that C items, dollar for dollar, hold up the value-creation process far in excess of their own value. These facts can be used to suggest a different approach to inventory turns and to measuring the waste arising from how inventory is managed (see Figure 7.1). Whether or not a company is using just-in-time (JIT) inventory methods, the A-B-C method still applies. In fact, it may become even more important as a tool to focus everyone's attention on the effectiveness of current inventory management policies.

While a broad range of counterbalancing costs and waste can be used to define the optimal level of inventory for each of the inventory classes (see Figure 7.2), at the raw materials level the effect of shortages on the value-creation process is dominant. The value-creating ability *"held hostage"* by a specific component or part is one factor that should drive these decisions. The "held hostage" measurement emphasizes the money that could be earned (the opportunity cost) and not the money that has been spent (a sunk cost). It keeps everyone concentrating on the primary mission: meeting customer needs every time, on time.

When attention turns to work-in-process and finished-goods inventories, the criteria for evaluating effective use of these "assets" (in other words, minimal waste) change. Each time these inventory levels grow, the company loses flexibility—the die is cast. The decision about what is going to be made and how it is going to be made is now irreversible.

The balance point for these two inventory groupings is between the capability of the company's processes (its internal lead time) and the variability of customer demand. If demand is highly variable in terms of timing (when finished goods are wanted), changing management

FIGURE 7.1   INVENTORY: A DIFFERENT LOOK AT TURNOVER

The traditional approach

$$\frac{\text{Cost of sales for the period}}{\text{Average inventory for the period}} = \text{Inventory turns}$$

Rule of thumb:
The more turns the better

Focusing on the profit potential

$$\frac{\text{Average inventory shortages}}{\text{Average inventory turns}} = \text{Inventory turn waste factor}$$

Rule of thumb:
The closer to zero the better

> **Doing this calculation by inventory class (e.g., A, B, or C) helps identify the profits held hostage by inventory management.**

without orders can create a high level of holding costs and risk of the OWEDs. On the other hand, if demand is highly variable in terms of volume (how much is wanted at one time), the company is trading off the purchase of excess surge capacity and its maintenance costs against holding costs and the potential of OWEDs-based costs.

All these factors have to be kept in mind when a company begins to set its inventory policies. If it can develop a highly flexible, responsive manufacturing capability, a company can drive its work-in-process and finished-goods inventories levels close to zero. The savings created by this flexibility exceed the decrease in OWEDs and carrying costs of inventory. This flexibility can provide for increases in service levels and responsiveness. If coupled with just-in-time inventory

FIGURE 7.2   INVENTORY MANAGEMENT: A BALANCING ACT

> **Excess inventory turns may result in foregone profits as shortages (inventory turn-based waste) pop up.**

Carrying costs

Foregone profits
on excess capital
tied up in inventory

Inventory turn waste factor
× the average profit per
unit produced and sold

Balancing these forms of waste is the goal.
More turns are not always better.

policies on A and some B item raw material inventories (holding more inventory) can improve a company's profit potential.

The effect of this increased flexibility on a company's ability to create value for customers can be seen at the Allen Bradley facility in Milwaukee, Wisconsin. Using state-of-the-art manufacturing methods (computer-integrated manufacturing, or CIM), Allen Bradley has been able to create a manufacturing process that can take orders for goods electronically, enter them into the production schedule the same day they are received, make them, and ship them—all within twenty-four hours of the customer's original request. Flexible production provides the basis for superior service. What waste is generated in this setting? Close to none. Using careful raw materials inventory management policies, the company is able to minimize all forms of inventory-based waste while providing the goods customers want when they want them. Removing waste from the production system has allowed this company to maximize profits and minimize inventory costs, while providing a service level in excess of that available from its competitors.

The "asset" at Allen Bradley is not inventory but productive capability that allows it to eliminate work-in-process and finished-goods inventories. The company "inventories" the ability to make its products on an "as demanded" basis. This asset won't show up in the accounting records, but it is the basis for every dollar of value created by this innovative, well-managed firm.

Inventory as a Liability, or Where's the Waste?

Inventory turns do not provide any information on the level of waste embedded in inventory management techniques. What types of waste does inventory create? Outside of the commonly recognized problems of obsolescence, damages, and shortages, there are a host of hidden costs of inventory. The first one that normally comes to mind is the carrying cost of having inventory. Carrying costs—or the combination of interest expenses to finance the inventory, space to house it in, insurance to protect it, and so on—are actually buried in many different places in the accounting system.

For instance, the interest cost for holding inventory is hidden in the general interest cost for the company: it shows up below the gross margin in income statements and is summed for every type of interest-creating transaction the company undertakes. The accounting treatment of this waste, caused by inventory management policies, makes it disappear from view. Unless it is directly assigned to the people or departments who control the inventory and therefore cause the cost, this interest cost can grow unchecked.

Some companies do charge an interest expense to their plants, divisions, or business units. For instance, Labatt Breweries of Canada assesses an interest cost on all working capital invested, including a charge for inventories held, to each brewery and each division. Caterpillar not only charges interest expense on working capital to its operating divisions but also assesses an interest charge on all the assets held by the unit. Interest expense is the result of borrowing money to finance asset acquisitions. It seems only logical to assign this expense to the people who benefit from it. Even if the financial accounting system doesn't "allow" this treatment, internal reporting can.

One measure of the waste caused by inventory, then, is a simple interest calculation:

$$\text{Average inventory} \times \text{Cost of capital} = \text{Holding cost of inventory}$$

This is a measure that promotes minimizing inventories. Does it make sense to drive inventories to zero in every situation to avoid this cost? This is a hard question to answer unless other waste measures are also used to help managers assess the total cost of, and the tradeoffs involved in, their inventory policies.

If inventories are cut to the bone, and a company has not mastered the just-in-time production model, a new form of waste pops up: missed delivery dates. There are several ways this form of waste affects a company. In the short term, it loses the immediate access to cash flows that come from shipping an order and collecting cash from the customer. In the long run, poor delivery performance can result in permanent loss of business. The first of these wastes is fairly easy to measure; the second requires a bit more creativity.

The short-term cash-flow effects of missed deliveries result in a loss of interest income, or flexibility, for the company. Instead of having cash available, the company loses this revenue and cash for the duration of the "late" period. One measure of this loss would be

$$\frac{\text{Lost}}{\text{income}} = \frac{\text{Revenue}}{\text{delayed}} \times \frac{\text{Number of}}{\text{days of delay}} \times \frac{\text{Cost}}{\text{of capital}}$$

This income can never be recouped. The revenue probably will come in eventually, but the use of that money is lost for the period of the delay. The company's cost of capital (its average interest cost to obtain funds from the capital markets) is used as the basis for this calculation because the company will have to find other funds to pay its bills and reinvest in its future if revenues are delayed. If a company misses a lot of due dates, this can translate into a significant cost—all waste.

The second aspect of waste caused by late deliveries triggers a series of short-term and long-term events. First, if a company happens to be a JIT supplier, missing a due date can result in heavy fines. For instance, any supplier that shuts down an automobile plant for even a few hours has to pay the company for its labor costs and any other expenses it incurs due to the shortage. This is a hefty fine that can sink a small supplier. Very few suppliers shut down one of these plants more than once and survive to talk about it.

If the specter of JIT isn't hanging over a supplying company, the extra costs caused by expediting "hot" orders through the plant are an ever-present reminder of the cost of poor planning. When due dates are missed, all sorts of hurdles have to be jumped to move the product to the customer. "Re's" are created throughout the company, expediting costs are increased, and waste is created by interruptions, as suggested by Figure 7.3.

In total, all the costs caused by inventory represent a major risk to a company. It is a risk that is created by the potential for waste, both in the short term and the long term. These high levels of potential waste are only part of the problem, though. When a company keeps high inventory levels, it has to move, hold, count, tag, and perform countless accounting transactions. In addition, these inventories end up hiding underlying process problems, making them disappear under a mountain of action that creates as much waste as value. Only raw materials inventories, kept at the best possible level to ensure ongoing production and minimal cost, even begin to earn the name *asset*. Taking all these factors into account, it is clear that inventory is more of a liability than an asset, no matter what the accounting records may say.

Many "nonproduction" managers may feel that discussions of inventory have no value in their settings. But a service company has an inventory—people—that can create value if and only if its capability

FIGURE 7.3 INVENTORY SHORTAGES, LATE DELIVERIES, AND WASTE

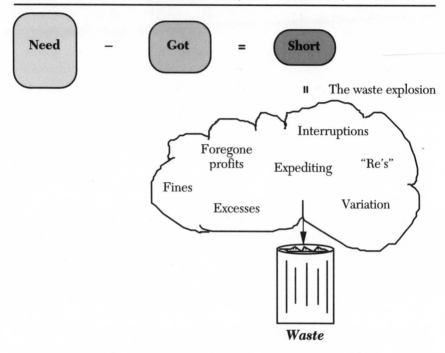

is maintained. A service company can create waste in the way it handles this raw material as easily as a manufacturing firm can. When attention turns to work-in-process and finished-goods inventories, once again a service company can find parallels. In fact, service companies are buried under work-in-process. It can be found everywhere—from the desks of individual employees to the engagements that make up ongoing operations. Finished goods, or the toolbag of services the company offers, have all the characteristics of physical inventory. Inventory, or the materials required to create value, come in many shapes and sizes. The question is not whether a company has inventory but simply how easy it is to see, touch, and manage.

ASSETS, ASSETS EVERYWHERE

The use of money is the only advantage there is in having it.

BENJAMIN FRANKLIN (4)

Inventory is one of the major assets found on the balance sheet for many companies, but it is not the only one. Cash, short- and long-term investments, accounts receivable, and property, plant, and equipment all carry the weighty title *asset* in accounting language. As with inventory, each of these assets is more a liability than a benefit if held in excess. Understanding the effect of excess assets on profitability, as well as the problems created when they are in short supply, provides the basis for capturing the value-creating ability of the firm.

Cash, Receivables, and the Operating Cycle

Cash is the basis for all business transactions. It is also the only essential ingredient for business survival; without cash the company fails—period. As history has shown us, in fact, a company can look very healthy in terms of the bottom line and end up in bankruptcy court. Running out of cash, whether it happens at home or at work, means running out of the ability to purchase basic necessities and to prosper.

Cash is both the starting and ending points of the value-creation, or operating, cycle. Cash is used to buy resources, which then are used to create the goods and services a customer requires, the sale of which creates accounting "revenues" and accounts receivable that can eventually be turned back into cash to start the whole process rolling again. The longer this operating cycle is, the more cash a company has to keep in its "inventory." Inventoried cash brings with it idle-capacity costs and the loss of potential value-creating opportunities, both forms of waste that seem to plague all assets.

The need to balance cash available with cash needed has been long recognized as the foundation for success in the business world. Many companies make profits simply by effectively managing their short-term cash balances, investing idle cash until it is absolutely needed. Often these "investments" are done on an overnight basis. Yet the result is impressive: interest revenues from careful cash management can offset interest expenses as well as support new value-creating efforts. Because this area is so well understood, only a few basic measures of waste need to be developed to illustrate the effect of long operating cycles on profitability.

Some of the basic measures used to evaluate the effectiveness of cash management include the following:

$$\frac{\text{Operating}}{\text{cycle}} = \frac{\text{Total days cycle to complete the value-creation}}{(\text{Cash} \rightarrow \text{Inventory} \rightarrow \text{Sales} \rightarrow \text{Cash})}$$

$$\frac{\text{Days cash}}{\text{on hand}} = \frac{\text{Daily cash expenses / Average daily}}{\text{cash balance}}$$

$$\text{Acid test ratio} = \text{Cash and cash equivalents / Short-term liabilities}$$

Each of these measures focuses on the "turns" of cash and not the waste created by poor management. Extending these measures to reflect the waste they can create yields a new set of measures:

$$\text{Profit potential ratio} = \text{Average profit / Dollar of sales}$$

$$\frac{\text{Foregone}}{\text{profits}} = \frac{\text{Operating}}{\text{cycle}} \times \frac{\text{Cash}}{\text{tied up}} \times \frac{\text{Profit}}{\text{potential ratio}}$$

$$\frac{\text{Foregone}}{\text{interest}} = \frac{[(\text{Operating cycle} \times \text{Average inventory and}}{\text{accounts receivable balances}) + \text{Foregone}}{\text{profits}] \times \text{Daily cost of capital}$$

$$\frac{\text{Idle}}{\text{cash costs}} = \frac{\text{Uninvested}}{\text{cash balance}} \times \frac{\text{Daily cost}}{\text{of capital}}$$

$$\frac{\text{Cash shortage}}{\text{cost}} = (\text{Cash needed} - \text{Cash available}) \times \frac{\text{Interest paid on}}{\text{short-term loans}}$$

The theme of these measures is simple: too much cash creates idleness costs, while too little creates excess interest expenses and the loss of potential profits because the company cannot take advantage of new opportunities as they arise.

Waste-based cash-management measures have an advantage over the more traditional ratios and analysis performed in this area: they put a dollar sign on the cost of ineffective management policies. This cost is a known factor in business, but a vague "days' cash on hand" takes on more meaning when an idle charge is attached to it. Aggressive cash management comes from understanding that idle cash or cash shortages both represent lost profits and diminished value-creating potential.

Another message the waste-based measures deliver is the impact of tying up cash in extended operating cycles. Accounts receivable may be classified as an asset, but it actually ties up the value-creating ability of the firm. Inventory, as we have seen, is definitely a waste-creating resource. Looking at the operating cycle from this perspective, it represents a drain on resources, lost opportunities, and excessive costs of doing business. The shorter the operating cycle, the better. If a company becomes very flexible and also manages its inventories and receivables effectively, it can receive the money on its sales before payment on the initial inventory purchases is due, resulting in a negative operating cycle. In this case, cash-based waste drops to the manageable level of idle capacity, an idleness that can be easily redeployed through a myriad of financial investment options.

Various cash discounts for early payment to a supplier on raw material and related resource costs may make the negative operating cycle difficult to achieve, but a company like Allen Bradley can probably come very close to this goal. Its manufacturing flexibility allows it to minimize the length of time cash is tied up inside the plant. Moreover, its good raw materials management policies and the extension of cash discounts for early payment on invoices by its customers create the potential for a two- to three-day operating cycle at this company. Freeing up cash from financing operations to financing growth is the ultimate goal.

Another Cut on Fixed Assets and Waste

The primary element of waste embedded in fixed assets is capacity loss, but there are also a host of other forms of waste generated by the way fixed assets are managed in a firm. The first of these wastes is the overproduction created by the belief that the best way to deal with fixed costs is to maximize production—whether or not the work completed adds value to the long-term bottom line. This tendency toward overproduction comes not from a complete analysis of the economic effect of make-work but rather from the information embedded in a basic accounting relationship:

$$\text{Average fixed cost per unit} = \frac{\text{Total fixed cost}}{\text{Units produced}}$$

What is in a formula? This accounting-based calculation, which reflects the basic elements of the theory of economies of scale, is driven by the recognition that the only way to minimize the ongoing cost of fixed assets on unit costs is to maximize their use. It is a logical conclusion driven by a focus on only one element of the total cost picture faced by a firm—fixed asset costs.

Thinking about how an asset can lose value (such as by being used, stored, or wasted), it is clear that the underlying assumption leading companies to place a premium on producing work-in-process and finished goods inventories that are not needed, is that these fixed assets lose value if not used. Logically, though, the value-creating ability of fixed assets *can* be stored. That is the reason they were originally placed in the "long-term assets" part of the balance sheet. The ongoing treatment of fixed assets as period expenses or as resources that are used up on a monthly basis appears to be due to an accounting preference for speeding the writedown of the asset's value through accelerated or time-based depreciation charges. This approach is driven by a concern for minimizing taxes, but its behavioral effect on the firm may well outweigh the tax advantage gained.

Applying a more natural logic to the way fixed asset values are consumed, it seems that each major fixed asset will support the value-creating efforts of the firm for a fixed number of activities or volumes. For instance, a machine on a plant floor is normally rated in terms of the number of cycles or uses it will provide before its performance deteriorates. This is the estimated useful life of this asset. If a company wanted to charge out the actual fixed asset value used up by production, it would probably use this unit-based depreciation charge. The result of this approach, called the *units of production* depreciation method, would be much different than the fixed charge currently used by most companies. Instead of promoting production at any cost, a units-of-production depreciation charge would encourage a focus on the other costs created by producing a product before its time.

Waste is created by the way a fixed asset is charged out to the outputs that benefit from it. The waste created includes excess inventory and its associated costs, increased move, queue, and setup costs, warehouse charges, increased material usage, increased risk of obsolescence or writedowns, and so on. Converting raw materials to finished goods simply to soften the impact of a period-driven depreciation charge on current product costs seems to be a worst-case example of confusing means with ends. The end desired is the effective, efficient production of goods valued by the customer. The means to accomplish this end is the use of various resources. To use resources to produce goods that aren't needed simply to absorb overhead doesn't make sense.

Stopping the waste caused by fixed asset depreciation charges is simple—convert to units of production depreciation. Whether the asset being used up is a computer, a punch press, or a delivery truck, the logic is simple: each time these assets are used, a small part of their future value-creating potential is used up. This slight shift in accounting treatment of fixed asset charges can shift management's attention to avoiding the risk and excess cost created by unnecessary production. A waste measure that can help promote this behavior follows:

Excess depreciation = Current depreciation charges
− Units of production
depreciation

Depreciation-based waste = (Excess depreciation + Waste
OWEDs-based waste + Excess
inventory carrying costs on
finished goods and work-in-
process) × Profit potential ratio

Excess depreciation charges drive a company to hold excess inventories, which creates excess inventory carrying costs and all the related
woes created when inventory sits idle, creating waste. If fixed charges
create this behavior, then its effect on the profit potential of the
company has to be detailed.

The question that may accompany this question is, "What about the
tax consequences of this change? Isn't paying excess taxes a form of
waste?" Excesses are waste. But the decision to use units-of-
production depreciation for management purposes does not mean
that this approach has to be used for tax purposes. The tax system in
the United States allows a company to use one method to charge out
depreciation for tax reporting and another for financial reporting.
There's no real reason to force the information used by managers into
boxes that fit a company's tax strategy. Changing the approach to
charging out depreciation is a win-win solution for a company.

EXPENSES THAT BUILD THE PROFIT POTENTIAL

*Take nothing on its looks; take everything on evidence. There's no better
rule.*

CHARLES DICKENS (8)
Great Expectations

In the same way that assets can actually end up creating excessive
expenses that reduce the value-creating potential of a firm, there are a
number of resources that are treated as expenses that actually create

long-term value for a company and its customers. For instance, people represent one of the major assets a company has at its command. Dollars spent on education and training of employees, treated as period expenses by the accounting system, are also asset creating. But labor and training are treated as expenses, not assets. In both these cases a period expense in accounting language is actually a long-term asset in the value-creation process.

Dollars spent on research and development also are expenses in accounting terms but are essential to the long-term health of a company. The costs incurred to create and maintain a company's core competencies can make or break the firm's future value-creating ability. The same logic is applicable to advertising, marketing, and related demand and image-producing expenditures; if they are foregone in hard times, there may be few goods times ahead. Finally, the dollars a company spends on environmental protection and building its reputation as a good corporate citizen create a series of long-term value-creating capabilities for the organization that may be hard to measure but whose benefit is seen every day.

The accounting term used to describe these expenditures is *discretionary expense*. This is strong language, suggesting that these are costs a company can do away with at will. While physically this may be true, these expenses are among the most important ones a company incurs. Falling directly behind current operating costs in terms of value-creating potential, these "discretionary expenses" are anything but optional if a company wants to prosper in the long term. If this fact is not recognized in some way within the measurement system of an organization, these vital uses of company funds can be curtailed just when they are needed the most: when profits are down or long-term survival is in question.

Measuring the waste created by excessive cutting of these expenditures requires a careful analysis of the long-term profit potential they represent (see Figure 7.4). This is one of the softest waste numbers created, but its behavioral effect on spending patterns and attitudes makes it an essential one. The key to gaining acceptance for this

FIGURE 7.4   MEASURING ORGANIZATIONAL "HEALTH"

Organizational Health Scorecard

Customer satisfaction index

Employee satisfaction index

Company reputation

Financial health

Brand health and image

Product quality and value

New product performance

Flexibility and responsiveness

Putting numbers on these "unmeasurables" is the key to long-term survival.

number is to include management in the process of defining it and determining how it will be reported. The softer a number becomes, the more important it becomes to gain acceptance for its use, as well as its core definition, before it shows up on a report.

Monitoring Expenses for Effectiveness

Stating that these expenses are value creating does not mean that spending in these areas is to be done without keeping a close watch on its effectiveness. For instance, if research and development expenditures fail to yield marketable new products for a company, they have far less value-creating potential than if commercially successful ventures are created. 3M Corporation is the benchmark firm in this area. 3M successfully transforms more of the work done in its research labs to commercially successful products than any other company in the world. When asked how this success level is attained and maintained, company spokespeople note that it comes from the way these projects are managed. As soon as a potential application for a new technology, product, or process is developed, a business unit is created around it. The resources and commitment necessary to make the product a success are dedicated to the project as soon as possible. This is, in one respect, a major risk for the company and the managers involved. But it is a risk that continues to pay off for the company in sustainable profits.

Ben & Jerry's is a well-known example of the power that can come from effective employee management policies. Rather than focusing on the "cost" of labor and seeking to minimize this expense, this company emphasizes helping its people grow and prosper. The results of this policy have been phenomenal: the company has grown from a small entrepreneurial venture to the point where its founders feel they can no longer manage it.

One of the key elements of Toyota's strategy for the future also lies in the ongoing development and training of its employees. Toyota does not treat this expense as discretionary; regardless of what the accounting rules may say, the management of this internationally recognized industry leader knows that its ultimate value in the long term depends on having people who are well trained, competent, and willing to accept new challenges.

Many of the forms of waste that are discussed throughout this book have their root cause in poor training of the people who do the work that creates value for customers. Tallying up the waste created by this decision is easy: sum all the waste identified in the company. Waste is created by a lack of knowledge, which can lead to ineffective decision making, errors, rework, and every other form of "re's," excesses, "un's," variations, complexity costs, and inefficiencies. Eliminating this waste may start with measuring it, but actually avoiding these profit-robbing costs requires knowledgeable people who are given the resources (physical and educational) necessary to succeed. Treating people as expenses or liabilities to be eliminated from the organization may be the most damaging form of waste a company experiences.

A Strategy for Growth

The goal in developing measurements that focus attention on eliminating waste is not only to drop more profits through to the bottom line but also to provide a company with the funds it needs to support continuous improvement of its core competencies. These core competencies—which build from the capabilities of its people, research and development efforts, and related "discretionary" items— are the basis for long-term profitability and growth. Inadequate spending on these items can send a company into a fatal tailspin.

A strategy for growth builds from a recognition that measurements are not all that matters. In fact, the only reason to use measurements at all is to direct attention and shape behavior. The numbers used by a company, which serve as a form of shorthand for defining and focusing the ongoing efforts of its people, cannot replace vision or values as the driving force of organizational actions. Numbers that focus attention on the right things and that help people see opportunities for improvement are better than numbers that hide these opportunities, but no number can replace good people who know the business and are working to sustain the company's value-creating potential. In the long run, this is the only capability that matters.

THE LANGUAGE OF ACCOUNTING: FINAL THOUGHTS

The limits of my language stand for the limits of my world.

LUDWIG WITTGENSTEIN (1)

Accounting is a language that serves many uses in the business world. It is an accepted shorthand for explaining results, focusing efforts, and setting objectives. As with all languages, though, accounting constrains the very world it attempts to describe. Using powerful words such as *asset* and *liability* to define the various resources and obligations of the firm, accounting creates a world of illusions. Managers talk of "managing costs" and "building revenues" as though these terms are nouns that can be acted upon.

Language hides as much as it reveals. Language shapes people's perceptions of reality and defines the actions they take. Language has more power to shape the future than any number or idea because it makes these concepts concrete. The language called *accounting* has all of these powers. Resources called *assets* by the accounting language are perceived, and managed, differently than those called *liabilities* or *expenses*. The former is cherished, representing the future value-creating ability of the firm. The latter terms capture the negative side of value creation; they detail the use of resources by the organization.

The objective of this chapter has been simple: to illustrate the distortions embedded in the accounting language and the behavioral effects of these distortions. Because accounting terms and logic serve as the basis for action in an organization, they must reflect the true impact of actions and results on a company's long-term value-creating ability—its profit potential. As we have seen, inventories are more of a liability than an asset; while many "expenses" (such as marketing, research and development, and training) are crucial to defining a company's profit potential.

Words drive behavior. Adding waste-based terms to the existing accounting language is one way a company can reverse the negative effect of accounting terms on management behavior. If accounting defines a resource as an asset, it must provide long-term value-creating ability to the organization in excess of the waste created by holding it. If accounting defines a resource as a period expense or a discretionary expense, the resource must truly lose all future value-creating ability by month end. This clear mapping of terms to business reality is a baseline for defining value-added accounting. If accounting fails this test, then it needs to be changed or reduced in status as the basis for measurements in the firm.

Building its long-term value-creating ability, or profit potential, is the ultimate objective of any company. The language and measurements used to describe its actions and results must clearly identify their positive and negative effects. If a resource is called an *asset*, it must plainly and unarguably be one. If a resource creates more waste than value, it is a *liability*, or drain on the profit potential. The power of accounting as a shorthand language has to be balanced against the waste it creates. Achieving this balance has to be the goal of every organization and every manager because it is the foundation for future growth.

For the highest task of intelligence is to grasp and recognize genuine opportunity, possibility.

JOHN DEWEY
Human Nature and Conduct (1)

CHAPTER 8

The Hidden Costs of Quality

*Aim at perfection in everything, though in most things it is unattainable.
However, they who aim at it, and persevere, will come much nearer to it
than those whose laziness and despondency make them give it up as
unattainable.*

LORD CHESTERFIELD (4)

The impact of quality failures on a company's profitability has received a good deal of attention over the last decade. With all of the
work that has been completed, it is hard to think that any new
information or measures can be added in this area. While this may be
true at a conceptual level, measuring the financial impact of quality
failures is still in its infancy. Financial or "cost-of-quality" reports
initially were developed in the mid-1980s and have undergone few
adjustments since then. The basic elements of a cost-of-quality report
include the costs incurred by a company for prevention of defects,
detection of defects, internal failures, and external product or service
failures (see Figure 8.1).

Companies have found that cost-of-quality reports can be good

FIGURE 8.1   MEASURING THE "COST" OF QUALITY

General Machining Corporation

Cost of Quality Report

For the year ending 12/31/95

Prevention costs		Total $'s	% of Total
Training	$ 25,000		
Design for manufacturability programs	40,000		
Stress testing	50,000		
Vendor certification	25,000		
Total prevention costs		$ 140,000	3.2%
Detection costs			
Inspection labor	$ 225,000		
Inspection tools and equipment	75,000		
Inspection supplies	50,000		
In-line imagers and defect detectors	500,000		
Total detection costs		850,000	19.8%
Internal failure costs			
Scrap	$1,000,000		
Rework	750,000		
Reinspection	125,000		
Rework machines and tooling	75,000		
Total internal failure costs		1,950,000	45.5%
External failure costs			
Warranty expense	$ 350,000		
Repairs-labor and expense	300,000		
Repair parts/replacements	200,000		
Product returns	500,000		
Total external failure costs		1.350,000	31.5%
Total cost of quality		**$4,290,000**	**100.0%**

attention getters that motivate management to invest money in preventing errors, thereby avoiding, the cost of fixing them. On an ongoing basis, though, few companies have found that ongoing reporting of the cost of quality is truly beneficial: a once-a-year review of these numbers appears to be adequate. In most companies, ongoing reporting of quality performance remains at the operational level; financial issues are not given the same attention.

One explanation for this apparent neglect of financial estimates is that the numbers being used to create the cost-of-quality reports are derived from the company's general ledger: they detail money that already has been spent. Management, though, is actively trying to minimize the impact of defects on the company on an ongoing basis. This effort requires before-the-fact or *ex ante* information on the potential profit outcome of a quality-improvement project and not after-the-fact scorekeeping. Traditional cost-of-quality reporting is simply not detailed enough, timely, or useful in preventing errors.

Effective quality reporting has to address several weaknesses of the current cost-of-quality approach:

- The information has to be available before a decision is made or an action is taken;

- The estimates of cost and potential waste have to include as much of the total effect of failures as possible: leaving out costs because they are not measurable in accounting terms is an undesirable practice;

- The information has to build in the actual cost-creating effect of the various types of quality-based expenditures;

- The information has to drive ongoing behavior at the operational level.

The last point is the easiest to address. To drive behavior at the point of action, quality cost estimates simply have to be available. If people know they are throwing away $100 every time they make a mistake, they are more likely to try to avoid making one. While people may know that a defect costs money, giving a good estimate of this cost to the people who can stop the defect is the only way to communicate that waste robs a company of its profit potential.

What is the cost of a defect? It is not only the materials scrapped in the process but also the cost for rework, reinspection, retagging, resetting up machines, lost value added, and so on. Beyond these financial costs, a defect negatively affects morale. A quick trip through any company that is experiencing high defect levels reveals a simple fact: people hate to do work that ends up in the trash bin.

At Bradford Soap Works, a casual attitude is taken toward low first-pass yields by management because the "defects" are easily reworked. Because the flashing around individual bars of soap is created as a natural part of pressing the bars and has to be recycled, adding a few bars with marred surfaces or other visible problems to this returning flow is seen as a least-cost solution for the company. Yet when a production line isn't running well and employees have to offload problem bars or toss them back into the process, they react physically. Normally mild-mannered employees begin to fling the bars into the rework bins in anger and frustration. They know that they are creating waste, and they're not happy about it. If people on the plant floor know this, so should everyone else. Putting a cost on defects is one way to convey this information.

DETECTING WASTE ISN'T PREVENTING IT

It is reasonable to have perfection in our eye that we may always advance toward it, though we know it can never be reached.

SAMUEL JOHNSON (4)

In a cost-of-quality report, preventing and detecting errors are bundled together as "good" costs that help a company eliminate the waste caused by defects. These costs are then compared to the cost of failures, resulting in a graphical portrait of the tradeoffs between these two types of quality expenditures (see Figure 8.2). The fact that a dollar spent to prevent mistakes yields more benefit than a dollar spent in fixing them is represented in this diagram by the use of nonlinear (curved) lines. The message delivered is clear: reducing failure-based quality costs improves profitability.

Thinking through the classification of quality costs, and their actual impact on the firm's profitability, it seems strange to bundle the expenses for finding mistakes (detection) with those that prevent the error in the first place. Prevention means no error will take place; detection suggests that it will, but that the defects can be sorted out in some way. Which is better? Clearly, preventing mistakes prevents waste. Detecting mistakes may keep them from reaching the customer, but the waste meter has already begun ticking at this point. Once again, the way this cost is treated seems to have tremendous behavioral implications.

It seems more logical to put detection costs into the "failures" bucket; any money spent here is a form of waste. This may seem like splitting hairs, but the issue at stake is one of images and perceptions and not numbers per se. When the objective is eliminating waste wherever it occurs, dollars spent sorting good output from bad cannot be defined as "conformance" costs. They are due to nonconformance: assuming that mistakes are a way of life is the only justification for charging the costs of sorting good product from bad to any place but waste. These costs belong in the "nonconformance" area of any report on quality costs—in the bucket of waste, not value added.

Good Costs Versus Bad Costs

When a company is attempting to develop its quality competencies, it often forgets that the only "good" quality costs are those that eliminate this form of waste from the process and product. Eliminating quality-based waste starts with the design of the product and follows the

FIGURE 8.2 CHARTING THE COST OF QUALITY

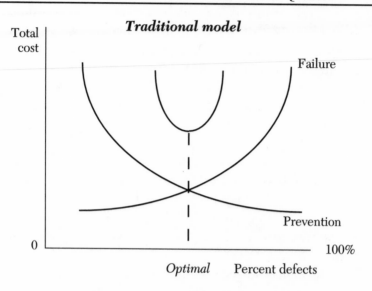

Traditional model

Total cost

Failure

Prevention

0

Optimal   Percent defects   100%

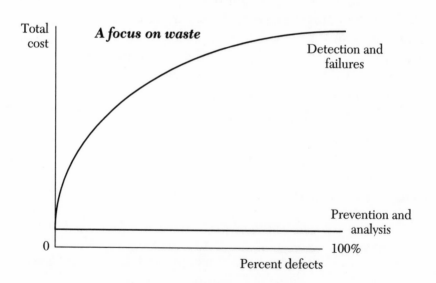

A focus on waste

Total cost

Detection and failures

Prevention and analysis

0   Percent defects   100%

product all the way to the plant floor as workers are trained and processes stabilized to ensure zero-defect performance.

A quality competency is built on understanding how mistakes affect the total process and product—not just the effort at one workstation or one process. When the total effort of the company is considered, decisions can be made to incorporate more expensive materials and processes than necessary to ensure that no problems occur downstream. On the other hand, when a piecemeal approach is taken to quality, cost minimization takes an illogical bent. Pennies are saved in one area, only to be thrown away in another. Since the dollars thrown away in one department are not traced back to their origin—whether the design of the product, its materials, or the preceding processes—these losses continue. A quality competence is driven by a recognition that preventing mistakes is the only acceptable approach to managing a business.

Some costs are incurred in sorting good product from bad to ensure that, to the extent that no errors are made in the inspection process, only good products make it to the customer. It may seem that spending money here is better than spending it even later on fixing a mistake, but once again, the downstream costs of fixing internal and external defects cannot be eliminated by simply discovering that the defect is there. Recognizing that one has made a mistake today does not ensure that another will not be made tomorrow. The gap between these two events is the key issue in understanding the cost of quality.

Learning from Mistakes: The Value in Detection

If sorting good units from bad units is the only role of inspection, it adds little ongoing value to the company. It may be the least-cost solution to a quality problem once it exists, but finding and fixing defects are not the goals. Defects occur, however, and it doesn't make sense to pass them through to customers, whether that customer is the next person in line or the final customer. So what is to be done about this "non-value-added but required" cost? One solution is simply to accept it and ensure that every dollar spent in this manner decreases the number of defects that are passed along. That is one solution.

What if a defect becomes the basis for learning, though? Finding a defect in this situation becomes an activity undertaken to help a company learn to do its work better. Defects provide a window into the production process—one that sheds light on inconsistencies, variability, and all the other waste-creating events that can be hidden from view. The expense of finding a defect that helps eliminate error from the process is value adding: it is part of the preventive activities of the firm. Understanding defects and tracing them back to their causes improves the quality competency of a firm. Rather than reacting to defects, this form of detection activity provides the basis for organizational learning and for reducing the potential to make mistakes in the future. In this setting, a defect is a gem and not a headache.

To measure the effectiveness of the "detection" phase of quality conformance, a company determines how many process and product changes, both current and future, result from the knowledge gained by analyzing a mistake. Several measures are suggested by this approach:

$$\text{Detection-based value} = \frac{\text{Errors analyzed and corrected}}{\text{Errors detected}}$$

$$\text{Detection-based waste} = \text{Detection costs} = \text{Detection-based value}$$

$$\text{Detection effectiveness} = \frac{\text{Downstream errors}}{\text{Total parts inspected}}$$

Detection costs that result in improvements create value and build the long-term quality competency of the firm. These are prevention costs; even though they occur after this particular mistake is made, they help the company avoid waste in the future. If the detection activities do not yield learning, then they are another form of waste— waste of potential knowledge necessary to build a company's ability to deliver defect-free products and services to its customers.

The ultimate waste, of course, occurs when the dollars are spent to "detect" errors and then errors remain undetected. Failing to detect the source of an error triggers a string of actions, lost value, and problems that can result in the loss of customer confidence and business. The detection-effectiveness measure captures this phenomenon and allows a company to develop an *estimate of the costs caused by poor detection.*

Detection activities, it seems, can be split into value-adding, non-value-adding but required, and waste-creating categories. To ensure that the dollars spent on quality efforts build the long-term value and quality competencies of the organization, management needs to know whether these costs improve future performance, not whether they fix problems that already have taken place. The key to sound quality information is its ability to predict and prevent future waste.

The Hidden Costs of Detection

Preventive quality costs focus on eliminating the need to inspect, sort, and correct defects. The failure to invest in this type of activity creates a range of actual and opportunity costs for a company. For instance, when defects are detected but are not analyzed for every bit of information they might provide about problems in existing processes and methods, an opportunity cost is incurred. The cost is the waste of defect-preventing knowledge. This opportunity cost shows up in the continued risk that this type of defect will occur again. Caught in a perpetual cycle of mistakes, a company that does not maximize what it learns from its defects is ensuring that it will incur waste in the future. This waste robs the company of its profit potential—the ability to create more value for more people.

The lost opportunities to invest in new value-creating efforts is one of the hidden elements of detection-based quality costs. Another hidden cost is any excess resource dedicated to detection in the future because errors are allowed to continue. Companies that have a high quality competency don't have to spend much money to find errors that don't exist. On the other hand, a company that fails to fix its quality problems continues to incur large quality expenses for detection and nonconformance activities. Any company that has to inspect every part produced recognizes that there has to be a better way to do business. That "better way" requires investing in knowledge about the process and the events that create variation within it. It is difficult to run a return-on-investment (ROI) calculation on this type of investment, yet it guarantees a high rate of return because each uncorrected error creates a cascade of waste. Waste avoided builds future profits just as surely as any other investment a company makes.

When an error remains undetected, it sends a ripple of variation throughout the rest of the organization. At every step of the process, work is slowed and adjustments are made to accommodate the variation the defect represents. Seldom are these adjustments or slowdowns monitored or reported; they are averaged in to the numbers used to evaluate the total efficiency of the work done in an area. This defect-driven variation may be hidden from view, but concealment doesn't lessen its effect on future profits. Like a slow leak in a tire, this undetected source of variation saps the organization's ability to respond to opportunities and to grow.

Of course, the hidden costs of detection activities don't end with those events that can be measured and analyzed. When detection is relied on to find errors, it creates a safety net for the organization that allows people to step away from their responsibilities to the customer. The attitude that "If I make a mistake, the inspector will catch it" is deadly. Perhaps the inspector will catch the error and perhaps not. Between the actual point of error and its "discovery," though, lies a wasteland. If any work is done on the product after the point of error, it is waste, regardless of how conscientiously the work is done. Ripples of variation are created that can trigger future errors, as machines and processes are "tweaked" to accommodate the error. Finally, the costs to detect and fix the problem emerge, like icing on a cake of mistakes.

The ultimate goal of dollars spent on conformance activities is to ensure that no defects occur and, if they do, that they are never passed on or ignored. This expenditure of scarce company resources has to build the *quality competence* of the firm. A quality competence is, at its essence, an awareness of how quality failures affect the future value-creating abilities of an organization. This consciousness has to be built into the daily efforts and attitudes of the people who perform the work and oversee its accuracy. Building a quality consciousness, and the acceptance of responsibility for it, is the key to a sustainable competitive advantage in the marketplace. Forfeiting this consciousness by lulling the organization into a belief that quality is something that is "inspected in" may be the most damaging form of waste a company can incur.

INTERNAL FAILURES: "RE'S" IN THE MAKING

To err is human, but when the eraser wears out ahead of the pencil, you're overdoing it.

J. JENKINS (2)

Internal failures trigger "re's" all over the place—some obvious, some not so obvious. An internal failure, or an error that is detected, usually leads to rework as everyone tries to salvage the part, product, or service delivered. Rework is 100 percent waste, but it is only the tip of the iceberg when it comes to the waste created by internal failures.

Most companies track the costs incurred in reworking defective units, but ripples of waste are generated by this unwanted intruder. Internal failures trigger the redoing of every activity and task that took place before the mistake was detected. These activities take place both on the plant floor and in the back office. Some are easy to see, and others are difficult to detect. In addition to these upstream "re's," an internal failure often creates downstream variation and an increased potential for external defects and the lost sales they create. To truly capture the costs of an internal failure, a company has to track and measure the waste it creates throughout the system.

The Visible Cost of Failure

A series of activities is the visible outcome of an internal failure: rework, reinspection, retagging, rescheduling, removing, scrapping, re-rework, reshipping, and so on. In addition, internal failures have to be physically rerouted throughout the entire production process. A company that set up a series of machining tasks only once before defects occurred may now have to set them up multiple times, once for each type of defective unit rerouted through the system. The visible costs of failure, then, are all the "re's" done to help the unit continue its path through the process, as well as the excess activities this secondary routing creates.

In most companies, the cost of internal failures is normally constrained to the rework costs. The logic here appears to be that it is a number that is easy to measure. Yet the other visible forms of waste created by the failure could easily be estimated. For instance, the cost for setting up machines additional times to accommodate the rerouted work can be easily calculated using the hours of setup time required (both for the failure and any work it interrupted) times the standard cost per hour of machine time. This is not the end of the setup cost, though, because the machine also could have been generating profit on other parts if it had not been reset to accommodate the defect: an opportunity cost for lost profits has been generated.

According to this logic, the hours spent rescheduling the work to move the product through the plant—the retagging, removing, and related "re's"—can all be placed in financial terms based on the cost per hour for doing that type of work. Obtaining these numbers simply requires keeping an "exception" tracking system that identifies the paperwork or parts that are being reworked, wherever they may go in the organization. Recording the time spent fixing a problem is straightforward if an exception reporting process is used. People have to track only the exceptions and not their ongoing work. Exception reporting is a valuable addition to the information toolkit of an organization.

To estimate the cost of an internal failure, then, a company has to develop a system to track the defect and the work it creates throughout the system. The dollars spent on rework are usually only a small percentage of the total costs caused by the defect. To summarize, then, the visible costs of an internal failure can be developed in the following way:

1. When a defect is detected, a tracking number is attached to it.

2. Each person who encounters this defect records the type and amount of effort required to fix it.

3. The hours spent are costed out using average hourly costs for that type of activity.

4. These various forms of waste are summarized into a total cost number.

What does this reporting process accomplish? Clearly, this information is not being collected before the mistake is made, so it is not going to prevent this form of waste from being incurred. Yet tracking the actual costs caused by an error can help a company develop a series of measurements and analysis to determine whether a defect should be fixed or scrapped. Here are several examples of these measures:

$$\text{Rework threshold} = \frac{\text{Potential profit from reworked unit}}{\text{Costs to fix and reroute the unit}} \quad \substack{\textit{should be} \\ \textit{greater} \\ \textit{than one}}$$

$$\text{Rework effectiveness} = \frac{\text{Profit from reworked units}}{\text{Total rework costs}}$$

$$\text{Rework efficiency} = \frac{\text{Total rework costs incurred per unit}}{\text{Average rework costs per unit}}$$

$$\text{Wasted rework} = \text{Total rework costs} + \text{Total value-added costs} \\ \text{for reworked units later scrapped} \\ + \text{Lost profits on these units}$$

The rework threshhold provides an alternative way to think about the decision to scrap a unit. Usually the decision to scrap is based on rules of thumb and instinct rather than economics. Of all the decisions made in the quality arena, however, this one has the greatest potential for robbing a company of its profit potential. Unless the reworked unit is going to generate more profits than it does costs, it makes no sense to rework it. Focusing on profits rather than the dollars spent to date on the units helps a company avoid the "sunk-cost" fallacy. The only viable basis for decision making is future costs and benefits—not past expenditures. What a company trades off when it fixes a defect is future profits: the dollars spent to create the defect cannot be recouped.

Having an economic guideline for making the decision whether to scrap a unit is an improvement, but a company also has to track whether its measures are working. The efficiency and effectiveness measures suggested above provide a way to verify that the rework threshhold is set at the right level. If rework costs, even after the establishment of guidelines based on the type of defect and its potential to create cost and waste in the organization, exceed the profits created by the reworked units, then the threshold needs to be raised. Measures that aren't adjusted and verified for accuracy can cause waste because they direct decision makers to the wrong conclusions.

The total visible waste created by a decision to rework an internal failure includes the cost of the work done before the defect is detected, the cost of the materials wasted, the traced costs triggered by the defect, the foregone profits caused by the redirection of company efforts to the reworked unit, and finally, the potential profits lost if the defective unit fails again. It is likely that the combination of these costs will tip the scale toward taking the defect out of the process completely. It shouldn't be thrown away or fixed, however: it should be studied. A defect is the key to better understanding the process and its potential for variation. *Reworking a defect increases the cost of doing business today at the same time it is throwing away the potential to prevent defects in the future.* The costs of internal failures, though, are not limited to activities that can be seen.

Back-Office Nightmares or As the Defect Turns

Often overlooked in the quality literature is the effect of defects on the back office. While everyone can see and understand how a defect affects a process and its efficiency, less thought is given to the waste generated as paperwork multiplies, customer complaints proliferate, and expediting becomes the order of the day. These invisible or "paperbound" costs of internal failures are no less important because they involve paperwork rather than the physical process. Waste is waste.

In a small company in Pennsylvania, the impact of internal failures on the back office became the source of conflict between management and its support group. Management, convinced that ongoing problems in material availability, late shipments, and customer satisfaction could be traced to the back office, began to reengineer this area. The starting point for this "fix" to the back office was the assumption that the individuals involved did not have the skills or desire to control the materials. Management, believing that it ran a fairly simple, repetitive process, could see no other explanation for the problems it was having in moving product out the door on time.

As successive layers of the organization were examined, the real culprit for these materials problems began to appear. First, the back office had not been computerized, which meant that every transaction had to be recorded and rerecorded by hand. While this paper-trained culture could handle the regular flow of work, it was ill equipped to handle the demands placed on it by rework and expedited orders. With only one set of procedures available to it, the back office rerouted rework and expedited orders through the same cumbersome procedures it used the first time it handled an order. If an order was divided into successively smaller orders because of defects, expediting requests, or delays and interruptions, new manufacturing orders were cut. One customer could, in reality, represent 100 orders, with over 1,000 parts, on 10,000 original manufacturing orders (M.O.s), and over 20,000 final manufacturing orders. If orders were rerouted more than once or interrupted more than once, the 10,000 M.O.s could turn into 50,000 M.O.s or more. What management saw as a simple, repetitive production process was a paperwork nightmare for the people trying to push an order through the system.

This company had a lot of heroes and a lot of villains. The heroes were the individuals who could push an order through the office and factory in spite of the process. These heroes were recognized and rewarded for their efforts. The villains, on the other hand, were seen as creating the crisis in the first place by not doing their jobs the right way or fast enough or accurately enough. If the villains could be replaced with more highly skilled professionals or a computer system could be found to compensate for their weaknesses, the company would succeed—or would it?

The true villains in this company weren't the people trying to handle the explosion of paperwork, but rather several bad habits the company—and its management—had acquired over time. The first bad habit was the unquestioned goal of meeting customer needs. How could this be a bad habit? The promise for performance was given without ever taking the time or effort to ensure the organization could meet these expectations. Process improvements were haphazard, and back-office support systems were never developed: the company could not deliver on its promises. Promises to fail are not what the customer wanted.

A second bad habit, following unrealistic ship dates, was that management interrupted the regular flow of work to respond to customer complaints. While the customer who complained might end up with the parts needed a little faster under this approach, the effect on the plant and the rest of the orders in-house was devastating. With schedules thrown to the wind and hot tickets attached to practically every order, came chaos. It was not a productive environment.

What did this chaos have to do with internal failures? Several issues are illustrated by the example. First, any internal failure would add another M.O. to the already confusing jumble of hot tickets and broken promises. In reality, though, the entire problem could be traced to internal failures, starting with failures in the development and application of back-office procedures, through defects in management policies in terms of unrealistic ship dates, and on into every activity and procedure used to handle paperwork. The paperwork stream itself was an internal failure, a defective process that created a defective product.

The invisible costs of internal failures, then, extend beyond the back-office activities created by the error (see Figure 8.3). They include the subsequent problems created by correcting the error, the proliferation of paperwork as the problem ripples through the system, the expediting of more and more work as the interruptions to the process take hold, and the loss of trust that inevitably takes place. In a culture of heroes, there have to be villains. That is perhaps the greatest waste of all.

FIGURE 8.3   THE INVISIBLE COSTS OF INTERNAL FAILURES

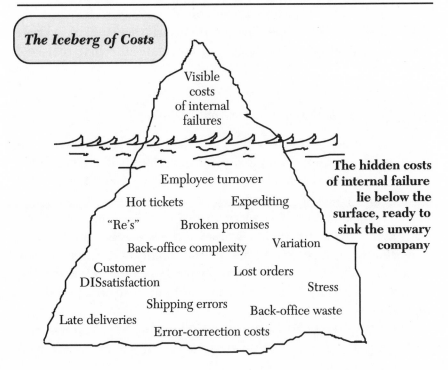

Can an economic cost be put on the waste created in the back office by internal failures? In some cases the answer is yes. A cost can be developed for the excess transactions created by rework and expediting activities. These estimates can help a company gauge its hidden costs, but it cannot completely capture them. In addition, material shortages caused by the need to rob materials from future orders to make up for units scrapped on current orders generate costs, but these costs turn up in terms of waste—wasted opportunities to generate profits that can be turned into future profit-creating potential.

The invisible, back-office costs of quality may be harder to measure and to understand, but they affect the organization as much, if not more, than the physical efforts that take place on the plant floor or in the field. Because the back office is so poorly measured and controlled by the accounting system, appearing as one flat overhead cost, uncovering the quality costs in this area can be a challenge. Yet it is a challenge worth meeting: future growth depends on support systems that operate effectively and efficiently the first time and every time.

The Downstream Effects of Internal Failures

The proliferation of fragmented orders and the related increases in the variation of production throughout the value chain are two of the downstream wastes created by internal failures. In addition, there is an increased risk of downstream failure from the reworked part. This downstream failure can take place inside the walls of the company or outside of it. In the first case, it is waste; in the latter case, this failure is a disaster that can destroy the long-term viability of the organization. A part that has been patched is simply not as reliable as one that has been made correctly the first time. This fact can come back to haunt an organization.

As the reworked part bumps its way through the production process, it triggers excess costs everywhere it comes to rest. Each handling of the part consumes resources, while each movement creates a paperwork trail that resonates in the back office. As rework clogs the system, outsourcing is turned to in an effort to offload the stress on the company. The outsourcing decision, though, creates more paperwork, more waste, and the potential for more defects. It is a solution that creates as many problems as it solves.

The cost of internal failures, then, is one of the major forms of waste a company can incur. While products with expensive materials may be worth the effort and expense to rework them, it is likely that even in these extreme settings the best decision a company can make is to learn as much as it can from the defect. Writing off the material and value-added components of a product's cost may seem like a drastic solution, but it is in all probability the least-cost solution for everyone involved. The combined total of visible and invisible costs of internal failures, whether in terms of services delivered or physical product shipped, are staggering. Unless a company is building atomic submarines, it simply makes more sense to learn what can be learned from the defect and move on. Any other decision will likely create waste.

EXTERNAL FAILURES: IT'S WHAT YOU DON'T SEE THAT HURTS YOU

The error of one moment becomes the sorrow of a whole life.

CHINESE PROVERB (1)

The last category of waste generated by quality problems is perhaps the most illusory cost of them all: the cost of external failures. What is an external failure? Quite simply, *it is a mistake your customers know about*. When the boundary between an internal mistake and an external one is crossed, the ramifications of the mistake grow exponentially. An external failure generates warranty costs and service costs, creates the potential for product liability, damages the company's reputation, and wipes out future sales.

Most of these "costs" cannot be measured by a traditional accounting system because they occur either in the future or outside the legal boundaries of the business entity. So the cost-of-quality report generated by the accounting group takes the easy way out. Warranty and field-service expenses—as well as returns, repairs, and replacements due to field failures—are pulled together into one number that is called the *external cost of failures*.

While these costs may be significant, it is unlikely that they are the major part of the waste created by external failures. Fixing a defective unit in the field isn't free, but it's the loss of future profit potential that really sets this type of quality failure apart from its cousins. Most of the waste created by external failures can't be seen or recorded today. It is, instead, a long-term form of waste that slowly eats away at sales and profits until neither is adequate to sustain the organization.

Polaroid Corporation is one company that is making efforts to model its external costs of quality. Polaroid, which follows a "razor-blade" strategy (cameras are sold at a minor loss, which is recouped through profits on film pack sales), knows that it has to sell four to five film packs to recoup the loss it incurs on a camera. If the camera or a film pack fails before this magic number is reached, the entire relationship with the customer is a loss.

Pursuing a razor-blade strategy has had many advantages for Polaroid, not the least of which has been to provide a basis for determining the cost of an external failure. For instance, if a camera fails early in its life cycle, the company loses an entire revenue stream. If the affected customer is one of the company's high-level users (fifty or more film packs per camera purchased), the company loses the profit on all the film not purchased. In some cases this loss is so significant that the company has instituted a policy to avoid it: immediate replacement of a failed camera at no charge to the customer. One phone call to a twenty-four-hour hotline triggers the shipment of a new camera by next-day mail. The only objective is to have the customer up and running again, using more film.

Where camera failures are the major concern for high-use customers, film pack failures are the key risk factor in Polaroid's traditional consumer markets. The logic here is that a customer who pays the price for a film pack and who relies on it to record a major life event (such as a wedding or first birthday) is so upset by a film pack failure that he or she often abandons the camera itself. What is lost to the customer is memories. What is lost to Polaroid is current and future profits. A razor-blade strategy turns deadly when the blades fail. The "razor," underpriced to trigger the initial customer purchase, isn't the key to a long-term relationship: the blade is. At Polaroid the real lesson embedded in external failures has been learned. Cameras and film packs can be replaced—customers can't.

Examples abound of companies that take the external costs of quality seriously, whether they can measure this form of waste or not. L. L. Bean, in Freeport, Maine, is a company built on a simple policy: if a customer is not satisfied with a product purchased from the company, the price will be cheerfully refunded, or the item will be replaced. Stories of hunting boots worn for fifteen years or more being replaced with a new pair, and similar stories that would turn the hair of most retailers white, are part of the folklore surrounding L. L. Bean. It appears to be a policy that works, for the company continues to thrive and grow as its ranks of loyal customers expand beyond the limits of the United States to Europe, Japan, and beyond.

For every external failure a company incurs, at least one future sale is lost. If the loss stopped there, it could be survived. But bad news travels fast and far. Common knowledge states that one dissatisfied customer will tell at least ten other people about any negative experiences with the company. If these ten people are then dissuaded from buying the company's products, there is an elevenfold loss of future profits from the one failure. It is a waste that continues to ripple long after the initial problem is forgotten.

Measuring the waste created by external failures starts with recognizing how lost sales affect future profits. Warranty and replacement costs are minor pieces of the puzzle. Extrapolating the loss of revenues and future value-creating ability triggered by an external failure is the essence of understanding and preventing this form of error and the waste it creates. The cost, in terms of lost opportunities and foregone profits, does not show up in the published financial statements of a company today, but it will show up downstream as revenues and profits slide.

Projecting the potential loss created by an external failure is a simple exercise that incorporates the following logic:

$$\frac{\text{Short-term}}{\text{external failure waste}} = \frac{\text{Warranty and repair costs} +}{(\text{Lost unit sales/customer} \times \text{Profit per unit})}$$

$$\frac{\text{Long-term}}{\text{external failure waste}} = \frac{(\text{Short-term costs} \times 10) +}{\text{Sacrificed value-creating ability}}$$

The first of these formulas can be calculated by most companies using current data on customer buying patterns under various conditions. To fail to generate this number because it hasn't been recorded in the general ledger can seriously impair a company's ability to control and improve its short-term performance. The second external failure measure is less concrete, but the message it delivers is even more important for a company to understand: short-term losses result in large long-term costs. The profits that would be generated by future sales are lost forever, along with their ability to support growth and long-term survival.

Whether internal to the firm or external, short-term or long-term, the insidious and hidden waste created by poor-quality service and production can dramatically impair a company's long-term growth and survival. It is a form of waste that most companies now recognize, but the full extent of its reach into the organization and its future is just beginning to be understood. Every dollar spent to prevent an error—to eliminate waste—will reap a thousandfold improvement in long-term performance. Every dollar spent to find defects, fix them, or to regain lost customer trust is waste. It is a simple rule that can shape a company's future.

The most effective way to ensure the value of the future is to confront the present courageously and constructively.

ROLLO MAY (1)

CHAPTER 9

When Illusions Become Reality: Outsourcing and Waste

The question is not whether to adjust or to rebel against reality, but, rather, how to discriminate between those realities that must be recognized as unalterable and those that we should continue to try to change however unyielding they may appear.

HELEN MERRELL LYND
On Shame and the Search for Identity (1)

One of the most challenging decisions made on an ongoing basis in a company is whether to outsource some of its work. These "make-versus-buy" decisions are driven by a concern for cost savings. If a company believes it can obtain a service, part, or product from the outside for less money than it would take to have the same level of work completed inside the organization, outsourcing takes place. If,

189

on the other hand, internal supply of the service or part appears to be the soundest economic and strategic position to take, then internal sourcing continues.

This decision looks almost too easy to justify an entire chapter. What could possibly be said about outsourcing that hasn't already been said? As with many of the familiar topics covered so far, make-versus-buy decisions are changed when waste and its impact on the profit potential are factored in. It's what isn't measured, not what is, that matters, both in the short run and the long run.

The numbers used to drive the make-versus-buy decision process are no different than the fully allocated, historical standard-cost numbers discussed in earlier chapters. The same flaws and concerns follow. But the underlying issues with outsourcing go beyond a concern about whether the cost numbers used to justify a decision represent avoidable costs. When a company chooses to outsource, it may be giving away its core competencies—its ability to create new products and new services in the future. With each loss of skill comes a diminishing of future profits. It is this message that matters in the end.

OUTSOURCING: WHERE SAVINGS END AND WASTE BEGINS

The handwriting on the wall may be a forgery.

RALPH HODGSON (2)

Reflecting a belief in the power of specialization to provide economies of scale, outsourcing decisions are at the heart of the economic puzzle that defines the boundaries of a firm. The basic premise of the outsourcing decision is that not all the skills necessary to make a product or provide a service are available in-house, or are economical to provide in-house. Promises of greater profits or of better use of the company's scarce resources draw a firm to outsourcing—buying from the market—some or all of its goods and services.

Not all business gurus have felt that outsourcing provides straightforward benefits. Henry Ford believed quite the opposite. In his design and building of the River Rouge facility, he relentlessly pursued the development of the on-site capability to produce a car from the making of the raw steel through the tightening of the last bolt on the finished automobile. In fact, he often decried the fact that he couldn't mine his own ore. Ford felt this was one remaining weakness of the River Rouge facility: it depended on outside sources of iron ore for its very existence.

Ford clearly understood the flip side of outsourcing that is seldom discussed in textbooks and articles on the topic: *outsourcing creates a dependence on the external market for the basic factors of production.* This dependence may or may not improve a company's long-term potential for sustainable growth; Ford seemed to believe it did not. Even today, Ford Motor Company continues to do more in-house sourcing than most of its competitors. Henry Ford's beliefs still overshadow the company's operations. Yet at Ford, too, the draw of offshore production has slowly pulled parts and products out of its domestic plants. In search of what is, at times, illusory savings, company after company shifts its basis of production to the land of "cheap" labor.

Outsourcing: The Critical Flaw

What drives most outsourcing decisions? The driving force is the belief that the labor savings or cost savings the decision will provide will net out to a positive profit for the company as a whole. Improving profitability is a logical goal in a capitalistic society, but the logic of this decision fades as the effect of avoided versus avoidable costs is taken into account. In addition to the "truth or consequences" issues that are an inherent part of the make-versus-buy decision, the underlying flaws in the numbers used to drive these decisions also play a part in turning projected savings into real losses (see Figure 9.1).

The critical flaw in most outsourcing decisions is their single-minded pursuit of labor savings. A holdover from the days when labor

FIGURE 9.1 OUTSOURCING: TRUTH OR CONSEQUENCES?

The "numbers" say . . . .

Labor savings (Projected labor reductions + Associated overhead) $ 800,000

Do It!!!!!

Reality is quite different, though . . . .

Labor savings – Actual avoided costs	$ 25,000
Increase in indirect costs – transferred labor	(300,000)
Avoided overhead	-0-
New costs:	
Increase in incoming inspection	(150,000)
Increase in engineering trips/costs to support vendor	(250,000)
Increase in investment for assets at vendor	(500,000)
Increase in working capital due to vendor/shipping lead times	(250,000)
Increase in incoming rework to adjust for new engineering change notices	(300,000)

Total savings (loss) from outsourcing decision ($1,725,000) LOSS!

192

represented a significant portion of a product's cost, labor-based arguments for outsourcing are based on shaky facts, figures, and assumptions. Some of the flaws embedded in many make-versus-buy decisions include the following beliefs:

- Eliminating labor will eliminate the overhead that is being absorbed on direct labor (the full-costing myth);

- The labor projected to be eliminated by outsourcing really disappears;

- The support activities needed to coordinate the newly created market transactions are relatively free to the organization;

- The basic skills and knowledge essential for future growth and prosperity won't be negatively affected by the decision;

- A part is a part is a part: outsourced items are equivalent in every way to products and services provided in-house;

- Any investment made to prepare the supplier to make the outsourced component is recouped in the savings, on a per part basis, that will result from the decision;

- All major costs are variable or semivariable and therefore can be cut away or eliminated easily once outsourcing takes place;

- The new supplier will be willing and able to provide the outsourced part or service for the long term at roughly the original quoted price and level of service;

- The time added to the production cycle or the inventory increases that accompany outsourcing are inconsequential when compared to the savings gained;

- Any decision that eliminates troublesome people problems from the company's list of woes is inherently a good one.

This list represents only a fraction of the underlying assumptions and beliefs that drive the outsourcing decision. Some of these statements are irritating and in many companies may be inaccurate. Yet each of these beliefs has been discussed at some time in some company that has decided to outsource part or all of its production. These points also appear when companies debate in retrospect why a decision made sense (a rationalization debate).

The first question raised in the above list is whether the promised savings from an outsourcing decision ever truly materialize. When outsourcing takes place, the only savings that can be claimed are those future costs that are truly avoided. So if labor is simply moved from the department that used to do the work to another part of the plant or office, there is no real savings. In fact, instead of incremental profits, what is generated is waste. The company keeps all its old costs and adds to them the value-added costs of the purchased part, increased inventory and shipping costs, and the costs to coordinate the external market transactions. In the long run, total costs of doing business go up under this scenario. The promised savings are illusory.

What if the people are eliminated once the outsourcing takes place? Isn't outsourcing logical if the company follows through on its plans to reduce its workforce? The answer to this question depends on whether the outsourcing was based on purely labor savings or labor plus overhead projections—a full-cost number. Logical or not, many times the decision to outsource is based on an accounting number that represents the "fully loaded" labor cost of current production. The assumption underlying the use of this number is that when labor goes away, the resources required to support that labor also will be reduced. The fully loaded labor cost, then, becomes a proxy for the total resources freed up by the decision.

Unfortunately, though, most of the support costs that are attached by the accounting system to a labor hour are not caused by labor. The resources that are used to support labor are normally fixed or semi-fixed in nature. Very few of these costs will "go away" in the way that the labor cost itself is eliminated. For instance, when one department in a plant is eliminated, the space that the department occupied remains. It is simply empty now: it has been transformed into waste.

In addition, The machines, indirect labor support, personnel and back-office support systems, and the general expenses of the plant all remain relatively untouched by the labor reduction.

The fixed costs of doing business roll on, only now there is less labor to absorb these costs. This fact sets in motion the death spiral, as overhead rates per remaining labor hour are ramped up to ensure that all the dollars spent within the four walls of the factory or office are charged to the customers and products that benefit from the use of these resources. It is of little consequence that these customers and products do not receive more value for the increased cost attached to them: the accounting ledgers balance, and the game continues.

While this statement may seem pessimistic, it is difficult to look at some of the outsourcing decisions being made by companies without skepticism and regret. The skepticism is driven by the fact that few, if any, of the projected savings in current costs are ever realized, while new costs pop up all over the place. Regretfully, the savings more often than not turn into losses. impairing the future health of the organization. This unfortunate and undesirable outcome results far too often when the effect of waste and its origin in unavoided costs are overlooked by the decision maker.

Old Costs and New Costs: Make Versus Buy Reversed

A medium-sized company in Cambridge, Massachusetts, is an excellent example of how wrong assumptions can lead to faulty make-versus-buy decisions and how an objective after-the-fact analysis of actual savings can reverse these decisions. Lifeline Corporation produces home health monitoring devices that are linked to a twenty-four-hour emergency service system. It is a well-run company that prides itself on the professionalism of its managers and its willingness to honestly assess its own performance.

In the mid- to late 1980s, Lifeline joined the long list of companies that decided to outsource their printed circuit board production to Asia based on projected labor savings. This decision led to several difficult years, as the company struggled with the realities of offshore

production. Faced with ever-changing product technologies and capabilities, Lifeline was in a continuous process of upscaling and improving its products. This logical competitive move affected the
stability of its demand for all its raw materials, including the circuit
boards coming from Asia. In addition, the company was a success.
Demand continued to outstrip supply, which led to a rapid increase in
the number of units the company produced.

Two very positive events, improved products and improved sales,
created a crisis for the company. While Lifeline could increase the
production in its own plant at will, it could not as easily increase its
circuit board supply. Penalties were charged to Lifeline if projected
production volumes were increased or decreased substantially. If the
company couldn't increase its order quantities fast enough to meet
demand, it could try to speed up the delivery of the boards already
completed. Rather than waiting for the circuit boards to arrive by
ship, Lifeline began to air freight boards to Cambridge to keep its
facility running at full speed.

As air freight bills began to pour in, other problems triggered by the
outsourcing decision also began to emerge. Most distressing of these,
from Lifeline's perspective, was the increasing level of rework that
was done when boards were received in the plant. Only a small
fraction of this rework was caused by poor quality from the supplier.
Most of the rework was driven by the product changes that were
taking place. Because of the time lag between production and delivery
of a circuit board and the relative inflexibility of the Asian supplier,
Lifeline was receiving circuit boards that already had been outdated
by product innovations. More and more time, both in the engineering
department and on the plant floor, was being spent putting patches on
the circuit boards from the Asian supplier to make them fit the latest
model of the product.

Lifeline was seeing, in real dollar terms, the proliferation of waste.
The waste that was visible was distressing, yet even these costs under-
stated the true economic impact of the outsourcing decision. Excess
freight, missed delivery dates, potential downstream quality problems
from patched circuit boards, excess inventories of obsolete boards,

rework, and all the back-office activities generated by these events were eating up profits today and presenting a risk of future loss of revenues.

Lifeline had an advantage over many firms that have ended up caught in the same lose-lose game. Because of its size and its culture, the company had little trouble reversing this outsourcing decision when its real economic and noneconomic impact on the company and its products became clear. Because the company produced only one basic product (with several models), management could separate the costs caused by the outsourcing decision from those not related to it. When the dollar signs were attached to the activities and problems that the outsourced boards caused, reversing the decision became the only alternative the company could pursue.

No one was made the scapegoat for this reversal of the outsourcing decision: everyone saw the folly of continuing a practice that did not benefit the company in the short run or the long run. Today the company continues to build its circuit boards in-house, honing its ability to respond to market changes as they occur. Lifeline is a company that has learned the truth, and consequences, of outsourcing decisions that fail to factor in the total costs they cause.

The Costs and Waste of Outsourcing

It seems that many of the savings that are projected to be the result of outsourcing are an illusion, while the new costs and waste created by this decision are all too real (see Figure 9.2). A company needs to understand and analyze the economic and noneconomic effects of outsourcing both before and after this decision is made. Several measurements can help companies understand the impact of a prior decision to outsource.

$$\text{Outsourcing effectiveness} = \frac{\text{Total cost before outsourcing}}{\text{Total cost after outsourcing}} \quad \substack{should\ be \\ greater \\ than\ one}$$

$$\frac{\text{Outsourcing}}{\text{waste}} = \frac{\text{Total cost after}}{\text{outsourcing}} - \frac{\text{Total cost before}}{\text{outsourcing}}$$

$$\frac{\text{Outsourcing}}{\text{productivity}} = \frac{\text{Output per person employed before outsourcing}}{\text{Output per person employed after outsourcing}}$$

$$\frac{\text{Outsourcing}}{\text{flexibility}} = \frac{\text{Days inventory on hand before outsourcing}}{\text{Days inventory on hand after outsourcing}}$$

$$\frac{\text{Lead time before outsourcing}}{\text{Lead time after outsourcing}}$$

New cost = Increases in air freight bills
"signals"

Increases in the soft costs in engineering, purchasing, or other back-office efforts

Increases in rework, incoming inspection, or other production costs

Increases in lead times required to respond to customer requests

Increases in travel, problem-solving efforts, rescheduling, reforecasting, or any other activity that can be tied directly to the outsourced part

All these measurements form part of the after-the-fact arsenal used to evaluate the effectiveness of the outsourcing decision.

Once the decision has been made, though, it can be costly to reverse it. What are some measures or issues that can be debated and explored before the decision is made? The list of these measures might include the following:

Avoidable cost = Actual resources that can and will be eliminated

New cost = Freight, rework, incoming inspection, increased inventories, potential penalties, air freight, on-site training at supplier, equipment at supplier, expediting, and all of the "re's" it would represent

$$\begin{array}{c} \text{New cost} \\ \text{impact} \end{array} = \begin{array}{c} \text{New} \\ \text{cost} \\ \text{(by category)} \end{array} \times \begin{array}{c} \text{Probability that} \\ \text{this type of} \\ \text{problem will occur} \end{array} \times \begin{array}{c} \text{Number of} \\ \text{times it} \\ \text{may occur} \end{array}$$

$$\begin{array}{c} \text{Total} \\ \text{new cost} \end{array} = \text{Summing of all new cost impact numbers}$$

$$\begin{array}{c} \text{Outsourcing} \\ \text{threshold} \end{array} = \frac{\text{Avoidable cost}}{\text{Total new costs}} \begin{array}{c} \textit{should be} \\ \textit{greater} \\ \textit{than one} \end{array}$$

FIGURE 9.2 THE OUTSOURCING GAME: EATING TOMORROW'S PROFITS

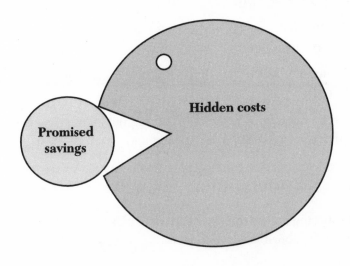

These measures point out that the key to successful outsourcing decisions lies in assessing their potential to create new costs and new forms of waste throughout the organization. If labor is not eliminated but rather transferred from one department to another, then this cost is not avoided; it is being turned into waste. These illusory labor "savings" turn into waste when viewed from the organization's perspective. Relatedly, if various overhead and support costs are not going away but in fact may actually increase, this information has to be faced in the beginning before the die is cast and the outsourcing efforts are set in motion.

When Outsourcing Makes Sense

It shouldn't be assumed that all outsourcing decisions are inherently flawed or that some benefits don't result from these decisions in many situations. In fact, there are some logical and valid reasons for outsourcing:

- The company doesn't have the capability to do the work;

- The outsourced work (heat treating or painting, for example) represents a significant investment in equipment and processes that cannot be fully used by the company;

- The outsourced work represents a health or safety risk the company is unwilling to accept;

- The quality of the outsourced part exceeds the company's own abilities;

- The technological advantages of the outsourced part or service provide a competitive advantage; and

- Outsourcing allows the company to invest its scarce resources in more profitable ways.

Outsourcing makes sense when it provides the company with more than a pure labor-based cost saving. If a company needs only ten hours of heat-treating capability in a week, it probably doesn't want to incur the expense and risk inherent in setting up an in-house heat-treating capability. And if a company doesn't currently have a painting facility capable of handling a new part or product, it may have to outsource this work because of its potential cost or the inability to obtain a permit from the Environmental Protection Agency to build a paint facility. A hospital may want to provide the latest technology to its doctors but be unable to fund or justify sole ownership of the necessary equipment, while a service organization may not be able to attract an individual with the requisite skills to do a certain job or have enough volume to keep this highly skilled individual busy.

Outsourcing has a time and a place, but that time and place is not when illusory savings are promised but rather when the company as a whole benefits from the decision. Any other basis for the outsourcing decision can actually impair the long-term viability of the organization, as layers upon layers of waste are built into its back-office procedures and the cost of the products and services it provides. This common decision is fraught with serious implications that often swamp any economic benefits it may provide.

CIRCUIT BOARD MYTHS AND THE GLOBAL MARKET

Reason is developed by going against habits and repetition; by following a legitimate whim; by not doing as others do.

A. R. ORAGE (1)

The Lifeline story is a common one in business today. Using an approach that might be called the circuit board myth, companies are shifting the production of this increasingly common component to companies and facilities far distant from the point of assembly and production of their major products. What are the basic elements of the circuit board myth? In essence, they are that

- Circuit boards are a commodity product with little or no competitive advantage;

- Global sourcing is the best solution to filling circuit board demand;

- Global sourcing is a least-cost solution to filling this demand; and

- The new costs created by outsourcing circuit boards are minimal compared to the costs and complexity of in-house production.

The circuit board myth is a reflection of many similar ideas surrounding the current wave of globalization taking place in the business world. Managers pursuing this myth and its promises are not naive or insane. They are highly intelligent people who make decisions about the future based on the information placed in front of them. It is the information being used that is flawed—not the decision makers.

Hidden Waste and Outsourcing

One company's experience with globalization provides a dramatic backdrop to the issues that lie beneath the surface of the circuit board myth. The company, a *Fortune* 500 producer of equipment for the photography industry, was facing a declining demand for its products in the United States. Management, seeing the writing on the wall, decided that the global marketplace would provide the solution to its current and projected economic problems. Following the logic that the key to future success was keeping volumes up, the company began pushing for sales of its products in South America, the emerging countries of the former Soviet Union, and related distant and underserviced markets.

Market penetration in these countries was good. Driven by bonuses that hinged on units sold, the salesforce traveled the world searching for new customers who would buy and use the company's products. Pursuing the belief that increasing volumes would result in increasing profits, the company threw its resources behind these new ventures. As the new business environment unfolded, though, this business-at-any-cost philosophy began to take its toll.

As was common in many secondary markets, the countries this company was beginning to do business with did not allow the direct transfer of currency or profits out of their borders. The only way profits could be taken out was in terms of value added—labor and conversion completed within the country. To extract these profits, the decision was made to place circuit board production plants in each of the countries that prohibited the removal of profits: the company's strategy was to use the value added in circuit board production to offset the unrecoverable profits resulting from camera and film sales in each of the host countries. This unique form of bartering was seen as a good strategic and economic move, at least in its early stages.

As the global sourcing network developed, though, the hidden waste created by the sales incentive system and the company's sourcing policies began to emerge. First, the company made large initial investments in equipment and management skills in the new production facilities. Second, it coordinated the supply of raw materials, mainly coming from several Asian component manufacturers, with the demands at the scattered production sites. Third, longer lead times were built into all the company's planning models, placing increased pressure on the marketing group to improve the accuracy of its forecasts. Fourth, major increases in both marine and air freight appeared as parts were ferried across major distances and circuit boards moved back to one of the two assembly plants in Europe and the United States.

The costs and consequences of globalization didn't stop here. Bit by bit, more and more support costs were created as the inevitable changes in market forecasts occurred. The marketing department could not project exactly what units it would sell over nine months from today, yet with a six-month supply channel for the circuit boards alone, this was the feat it was expected to accomplish. The result was increasingly frequent forecast changes, which increased support costs and damaged existing relationships between marketing and the rest of the organization. Faced with the chaos that is created when long lead times are combined with uncertain demand, the company struggled to balance production, respond to emergencies, and fire-fight its way to economic success.

As the fight waged on, all eyes turned toward the performance of the domestic circuit board plant and its impact on profitability. First, it was a visible cost, and second, the domestic plant was absorbing the cost of coordinating the global network. The result was that the "prices" quoted by the domestic plant soared, making it look like the high-cost producer of what was, at times, the low-quality product.

When the veil was stripped away, though, the traceable, production-caused costs in this plant were highly competitive with the best of the external suppliers of circuit boards. In addition, the domestic plant was absorbing all the uncertainty in the supply chain: shortages and overages ended up in this plant. It was called on to produce new products, old products, small runs, and big runs—all on a moment's notice. The obvious result of responding to these many and varied demands was increased costs and a higher level of error as the workforce and equipment were pushed to their limits to absorb variety effectively and efficiently. Bit by bit, repetitive production was removed from the plant, and bit by bit its performance against the company's defined measurements deteriorated. The plant was ultimately closed.

Did the company gain by this sequence of events? Ask the people who lost jobs in the process or who understood that the core problem was that the plant had become a shock absorber for the company. In closing the doors, the company avoided few if any of the current costs of making the circuit boards or supporting the global network. Instead, it incurred greater levels of waste and drove the increasing costs this plant had been absorbing deeper into the morass of overhead allocations and countercharges that proliferated in the firm.

The long-term prognosis for this organization is not good, but the moral this story represents extends beyond how bad decisions can be reinforced by bad numbers. Because there are so many hidden costs in globalization, the economic benefits of pursuing this path to improve performance have to be carefully and honestly assessed against its potential costs. Outsourcing, whether domestic or global, is not an absolute good. And when the outsourced good is a circuit board, whether it is designated a commodity or the differentiating feature of a product, downstream problems can be expected. Circuit boards, the brains of modern technology, are a primary cost driver in every organization that puts their power to use. Outsourcing of this "commodity" can prove to be a fatal decision.

OUTSOURCING THE FUTURE: CORE COMPETENCIES AND WASTE

No gain is so certain as that which proceeds from the economical use of what you already have.

LATIN PROVERB (4)

Another side of the complex issue of outsourcing is the outsourcing of core competencies. Both of the major examples explored in this chapter have involved circuit boards, but the decision to outsource involves far more than the boards that go into a product. Every day companies decide to buy key parts, whole units, and services that may or may not improve the company's value-creating ability.

Companies outsource their payroll functions, their distribution functions, their production of certain parts, or their ability to provide key services to patients or customers because the external supplier promises to perform this work better than the company can. When talking about a company's core competencies, though, these promises are not enough. A core competency, or the company's key value-creating ability, should never be up for bid or for debate. Core competencies are to be cherished and protected, not outsourced.

Honda: Core Competencies at Work

When most people think of Honda Corporation, they envision either a car or a motorcycle. At Honda, though, the focal point is the engine and not the products that engines end up in. Since its inception, Honda has known that what it does, and must continue to do, better than anyone else is to make engines that perform flawlessly with minimal repairs for an extended period of time.

Suggesting to Honda that it outsource the building of its engines or the components to its engines would be inconceivable. The company is built on engines and is in constant search of products its engines can be put into. There is no cost savings great enough to lead this company into abandoning its competitive advantage in the market in the long term.

Unfortunately, not every company is as aware of its core competencies and the effect of outsourcing them on long-term growth. Treated as just another feature of the company, a core competency is often up for bid. When current profits dominate the decision makers' minds, it seems to matter little how a decision to outsource affects a company's future.

What companies have outsourced their future? General Motors is one of the first companies to come to mind. Every part that goes into a GM car can end up being outsourced: there are no "competencies" being protected. This may sound harsh, but the recent decline in GM's competitiveness reflects its failure to focus on building a core competency and keeping it. Without this single-minded focus on what it does best, the company appears to be making its decisions based on their short-term effects on the bottom line.

The real danger of outsourcing is that in parceling out its knowledge about how to make a product or provide a service, a company may be sharing its secrets with a competitor or giving away the vital ingredients of its success. Polaroid Corporation refuses to share its "instant imaging" competency with anyone, while a sister company shares the basic workings of its cameras with the global marketplace. In the former situation, the value of a core competency is understood, while in the latter it is being ignored.

In the long term, all a company has to trade on is its core competencies. If these are outsourced, the company may limp along in the near future, but it jeopardizes its ability to respond to market shifts, to create new products and services, and to be flexible in the face of changing customer requirements.

Outsourcing Competencies: Examples and Concerns

Two examples of outsourcing of basic elements of companies' core competencies are the elimination of developmental editing at Major Books, Inc. Company and the premature substitution of flexible machining systems (FMS) for skilled machinists at Ingersoll Milling Company. In both of these cases, the driving force behind outsourcing has been perceived cost savings. Yet the long-term effect of these two illustrations of outsourcing is the potential loss of a key core competency of the firm.

Major Books, Inc. Company publishes a broad range of books, from popular trade books through college textbooks. Its primary market is in textbooks for kindergarten through twelfth grade. There are many reasons for the company's strengths in this market, including the maintenance of an up-to-date list of texts as well as the ability and willingness to pursue new ideas and new authors who seem to have a different, more effective way to approach traditional topics. The developmental approach for creating new products and a high-level market presence filters throughout the organization.

The college textbook segment of the company has been plagued with less than stellar performance over the past ten years. While it has pursued a developmental approach in this market segment equal to its primary and secondary school markets, the volatility of demand in the college segment, combined with increasing demands for high-cost support materials to accompany each new college text, has made its total performance lag management expectations. The inevitable result of this flagging performance has been the institution of various cost-reduction programs and decisions to outsource or eliminate many of the white-collar jobs traditionally completed by Major Books, Inc. employees.

One of the key tasks the company has decided to outsource in the college division is developmental editing. A developmental editor works with the authors of a textbook at each step of the writing and production process to ensure that the final product (a printed textbook) meets the company's stringent criteria for success. High-quality textbooks, with minimal printing and calculative errors, are the goal of this developmental process. Helping authors achieve this objective as quickly and smoothly as possible is the job of the developmental editor.

The use of developmental editors has, in the past, provided Major Books, Inc. with a competitive advantage in signing new authors, which has led to its ability to offer new textbooks and the potential to capture higher market-share levels with innovative approaches. This long-term, core-competency-building effort, though, provided little visible benefit to the company: management could not see the contributions of the developmental editor in dollars and cents. When cost cutting became a priority, this "nonessential" activity was discontinued.

The core competency of a textbook publisher would seem to be the ability to help a writer turn thoughts into sellable texts. This is the basis for all future sales. Eliminating this competency—or outsourcing it, if possible—suggests that the long-term yield on future projects may diminish. Rather than taking the 3M view of product development—namely, to support new projects fully from day one— Major Books, Inc. has made the decision to shift resources away from new project support. In the long run, this shift probably will mean that Major Books, Inc. will be able to sign fewer new authors. Fewer new authors eventually means declining sales. While it may be difficult to put a value on the competency created by the developmental editing activity today, the downstream implications of losing this basic skill are ominous. In a market where new ideas and approaches sell textbooks, both in terms of the basic technologies used to deliver education as well as the models that underlie these efforts, a company's ability to turn good ideas into sellable products may spell the difference between market dominance and being an "also ran." Only time will tell if Major Books, Inc.'s decision will have a happy or a sad ending.

Ingersoll Milling: When People Are a Competency, Not a Cost

Another company that appears to be giving away its core competency through outsourcing and changes in its management processes is Ingersoll Milling. Ingersoll Milling is a producer of machines used by other companies to make product. As part of the machine tool industry, Ingersoll has built a reputation on its ability to create unique function machines, on demand, for customers across the globe.

At Ingersoll, the key to its ability to meet or exceed customer requirements has always been its highly skilled workforce. As many companies have found out, no machine can replace a highly skilled and talented machinist when it comes to developing and building a new product or process. Yet in the late 1980s, Ingersoll began to lose its core competency—its machinists—due to a strategic decision to pursue the fast-growing flexible machining systems market.

Ingersoll's logic was that to effectively sell the FMS concept to its customers it had to use this technology within its own four walls. This management decision led the company to begin replacing its machinists with FMS centers and computer programmers. Bit by bit, the machinists' work was deskilled as they became observers rather than the drivers of the productive process. Fewer and fewer machinists were needed as the FMS centers developed.

This logical progression away from people and to machines might have made sense if Ingersoll's business was repetitive in nature. It wasn't. Almost every machine built by Ingersoll was unique. Using repetitive-based technologies (FMS) instead of flexible, talented

machinists began the decay of the company's core competency—its
ability to make one-of-a-kind machines better, faster, and cheaper
than the competition.

Is swapping machines for people outsourcing? If only a skilled
machinist can support the development of unique machines, and if a
machinist reading a blueprint is less costly than the computer pro-
gramming needed to create a code to make a part that will be produced only once, then the company has outsourced its ability to build
new machines on an "as needed" basis. To obtain this skill, Ingersoll
increasingly has to turn to the external market to buy the same skills
and abilities it used to have in-house. Once again, the jury is still out
on whether this outsourcing of a core competency will prove to be a
sustainable, beneficial decision in the long term.

WASTE AND CORE COMPETENCIES: A FINAL NOTE

In most sections of this book, waste has been defined, measured, and
explored. When dealing with the outsourcing of a core competency,
waste is all that remains in the company's future. What is wasted when
core competencies are outsourced is the company's future, its potential to create value, its knowledge, and the efforts of the people who
comprise it. There is no need to put a dollar sign or measure on this
type of waste: simply zero out the books and send everyone home.

The central message in the discussion of outsourcing is that in all
but a few cases, outsourcing is a dangerous choice that can negatively
affect a company's long-term profit potential (see Figure 9.3). Short-
term "savings" from outsourcing, whether this external sourcing is for
a peripheral part or a core competency, can be more illusion than fact.
In reality, most outsourcing decisions cause more cost than they save,
but these costs—this waste—is buried in the overhead accounts and
the allocations of these costs to products and services. Outsourcing is
one decision that may look good on paper but seldom generates the
benefits it promises.

The most common decision a company faces is whether to make

FIGURE 9.3   OUTSOURCING THE FUTURE

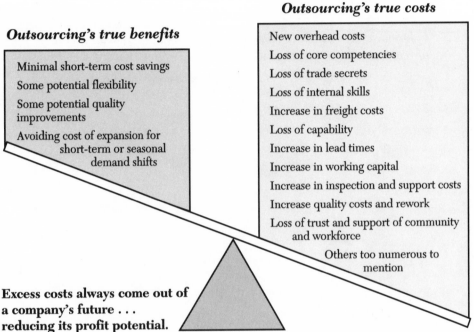

Outsourcing's true costs

Outsourcing's true benefits

Minimal short-term cost savings
Some potential flexibility
Some potential quality improvements
Avoiding cost of expansion for short-term or seasonal demand shifts

New overhead costs
Loss of core competencies
Loss of trade secrets
Loss of internal skills
Increase in freight costs
Loss of capability
Increase in lead times
Increase in working capital
Increase in inspection and support costs
Increase quality costs and rework
Loss of trust and support of community and workforce
Others too numerous to mention

Excess costs always come out of a company's future . . . reducing its profit potential.

or buy its parts, products, and services. It also is the most critical decision made. Auditing the actual benefits of an outsourcing decision, after it is made, is not an option; it has to be a rule. If outsourcing decisions continually fail to show the expected benefits, against any of the measures in the original justification or those suggested in this chapter, they have to be rescinded. To leave a bad decision alone, to let it fester, serves no one well in the long run.

Outsourcing brings with it a clear view of the implications of ignoring waste and its impact on an organization. Whether this outsourcing results in a decision to shift only a part of a company's production or to close entire plants, the underlying danger of hidden costs and sacrificed future potential to create value remain an ever-

constant reminder that what may seem simple (the outsourcing decision) may actually be quite complex. It's the costs that a company
doesn't see that hurt it.

> *In formal logic, a contradiction is a signal of a defeat; but in the evolution*
> *of real knowledge it marks the first step in progress toward a victory.*
>
> ALFRED NORTH WHITEHEAD (2)

CHAPTER 10

Making Waste Visible

Reason may fail you. If you are going to do anything with life, you have sometimes to move away from it, beyond all measurements. You must follow sometimes visions and dreams.

BEDE JARRETT
The House of Gold (1)

Making waste visible within an organization begins with accepting that waste, not cost, defines a company's long-term prospects. Separating waste from value-adding cost is the key to continuous improvement and to creating a sustainable competitive advantage in every organization, large or small, in the manufacturing or service sector. Only when waste is driven as close to zero as possible can a company reach its true profit potential.

In the preceding pages, waste has been defined, explored, and portrayed in measurement form across many organizational activities and situations. Waste has been found in the assumptions used to manage a business, the language of accounting used to describe it, and the tools and techniques that define daily activity in organizations. Waste begins to appear in an organization as soon as efficiency (doing things right) takes precedence over effectiveness (doing the right things). It continues to build, hidden from view, in actions and

213

decisions that are based on faulty assumptions or good intentions rather than on the careful analysis of the long-term implications they represent. This final chapter knits these concepts together into a strategy for eliminating waste.

ASSUMPTIONS, PRESUMPTIONS, AND WASTE

Our ideas are only intellectual instruments which we use to break into phenomena; we must change them when they have served their purpose, as we change a blunt lancet that we have used long enough.

CLAUDE BERNARD (8)

The key factors driving waste in any setting are the *assumptions* made by the people who are responsible for taking action. In the West, it generally has been assumed that understanding an organization begins with understanding its parts. This assumption has led to an intense focus on individual efficiencies rather than organizational effectiveness and on the output of one machine rather than the production of sellable units by a process designed to meet customer requirements. Coupling this "piecemeal" view of the world with a preoccupation with short-term results creates a wasteland of resources that rob a company of its profit potential.

In contrast, a systemic view of the organization combined with a focus on the effectiveness and efficiency of the processes used to create value in an organization provides a framework for action that does not assume waste is a natural part of doing business. When the entire organization's effectiveness in meeting customer requirements is the baseline for evaluating performance, waste and its effects become visible and actionable. Waste, or the loss of future opportunities to create value, emerges in this setting as the key to improving current and future results.

Waste is the invisible loss of value-creating ability, a loss that makes the organization less than the value of its parts (see Figure 10.1). It is a deadweight loss to the firm and to society. In a world of increasingly

FIGURE 10.1   THE DEADWEIGHT LOSS CALLED WASTE

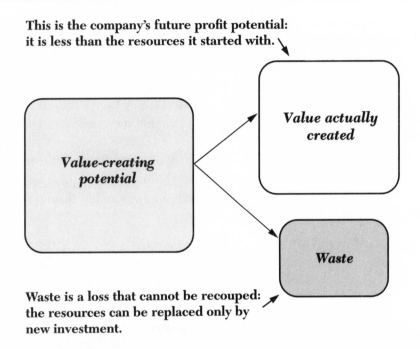

This is the company's future profit potential: it is less than the resources it started with.

Value-creating potential

Value actually created

Waste

Waste is a loss that cannot be recouped: the resources can be replaced only by new investment.

scarce resources and ongoing growth of total demand, this waste cannot be tolerated. Companies that continue to follow "tried and true" assumptions and work methods that focus on results and cost rather than on maximizing processes and eliminating waste from their daily activities are rapidly finding themselves in competitive deep waters without a life raft. Measuring, reporting, and eliminating waste give a company the ability to stay afloat and prosper in the unpredictable waters of global competition.

Efficiency, Effectiveness, and Waste

Efficiency-based measurement systems are a natural outcome of taking a piecemeal, or reductionist, view of the world. Since "doing the right thing" (or effectiveness) requires an understanding of the entire organization and its goals, it cannot shape action in an organization that is focused on evaluating the efforts of one part at a time. In fact, the most damaging of the assumptions embedded in most measurement systems is that effectiveness is assured if everyone does his or her job efficiently. Rather than providing a stable platform for future action, the act of assuming effectiveness into performance measures practically ensures its loss within an organization.

This unquestioned belief that effectiveness is being served when efficiency of a part of the organization is being measured has several implications:

- Resources are used efficiently, but the outcome of this usage is waste and not value creation. A company efficiently throws away its profit potential.

- Good people are directed to less than desirable activities. The ultimate outcome of this misdirection can be the elimination of good people whose jobs were built on waste.

- Efficiency in the short run results in long-term deterioration of a company's value-creating ability as waste proliferates.

- During cost-reduction drives, ineffective but efficient activities remain—reduced but not eliminated. Effective and efficient activities are also reduced in most cases, generating another form of waste.

- Individuals in the organization hear the message "All's well" from the performance-measurement system, while, in reality, the ship may be going down with all hands on board.

Believing that the organization is performing well, many managers who rely on efficiency-based reporting systems continue to support and encourage the creation of waste throughout their organizations.

Doing the wrong things really well is not a recipe for success: it is a guarantee of disaster. The global economy doesn't factor this type of waste into the price it sets for a good or service. The basis for price

setting on a global scale is "a reasonable profit"—not cost recovery for
the supplier. The waste created by ineffectiveness in a company is
paid for by its profits and its future growth. This loss cannot be
recouped in the future. Once a company gives away its value-creating
ability, it has to pay the capital markets dearly to replace it. Future
growth becomes dependent on the good wishes of the marketplace
rather than on the skill and knowledge of the organization and its
workforce.

Structural and Process-Driven Waste

While the basic assumptions used to manage and measure a firm's
performance are one source of waste, the way work is structured and
carried on also affects an organization's ability to create value for its
customers. The structure of an organization is a reflection of the assets
it controls and how it arranges these assets into activities, work centers, or processes. When a company structures its work, it is implicitly
defining the number, type, and amount of resources it will consume
every time it produces a good or service for a customer. This structure
also defines the number, type, and amount of resources used up
simply to coordinate the organization's activities.

Each resource has a defined capability to do work (a capacity) as
well as a preset purchase package and level of storability. Structuring
an organization to do work should start by examining how well resource capabilities are balanced within a process. Permanent structural waste is created whenever individual resource capability is not
matched to output demand or the capability of the bottleneck resource in the process. One measure of how well a system has been
designed is its level of structural waste.

Once a system is designed, the waste meter has only begun to tick.
A second layer of waste in an organization is driven by the use, or lack
of use, of the system and its capabilities. The system can be directed to
do value-adding work by its managers and can do it well. This is the
only way waste can be avoided within the organization. Under any
other condition—whether enforced idleness, "re"work of any type,

FIGURE 10.2 TRANSFORMING WASTE TO VALUE

Deflating the bag of waste . . .

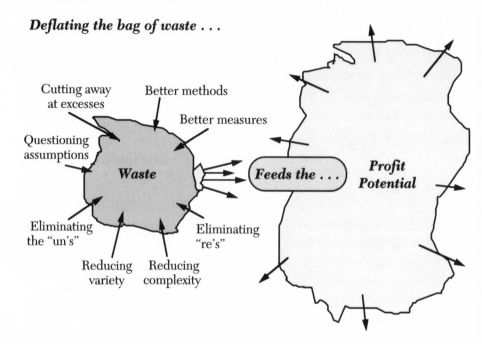

the performance of ineffective activities, inefficient efforts, or simply defective work—waste is being created (see Figure 10.2). This is the message delivered by a measurement system that captures waste and its impact on the organization's profit potential: waste is very hard to avoid.

Measuring Waste

While measurements do not make an organization successful, the lack of measurements can lead to floundering as managers struggle to find the "right" combination of products, services, and activities to maximize the firm's profits. Without measurements, a company cannot reliably detect and prevent disasters on the horizon. Without measurements of waste, decision makers cannot objectively analyze the tradeoffs between one course of action and another. Decisions are made using models that focus attention on only one part of the organization or a few of the areas affected by the decision. In other cases, instinct rules the day, as experience and hindsight replace an active and careful analysis of the relative cost and waste potential of each course of action open to the firm.

The reason to measure waste is that waste is an actionable characteristic of the process. Not only can individuals work to eliminate waste, but they are motivated to do so. Rather than pursuing a vague efficiency goal or juggling events to meet preset performance objectives, an individual who has been asked to help the company eliminate waste is on a mission. Eliminating waste is something people like to do; they understand why it is being done and can accept the decisions that result in its elimination.

Six basic types of waste were detailed in Chapter 3. The structural forms of waste, including excess resources built into the system's design, inadequate development of system capabilities (the "uns" or failure to load the software needed to drive the hardware of the system), and uncontrolled system complexity were explored. On the process or use side of the waste equation, the dominant issues discussed were the "re's" (doing something repeatedly when value is created only the first time an activity is done), interrupts, and variation in how work is done. These six basic causes of waste can be found in every organization, regardless of the type of activities it performs or the goods and services it provides to its customers.

Several different measurement approaches for capturing how these various forms of waste affect the organization were detailed in Chapter 2: percentage change measurements, gap measures, ratio measures, summary measures, and relative percentage measures. Decisions about the types of measurements and when, where, and why they are used depend on the behavioral effect the measure is supposed to have. Recognizing that the basic rule of management is that *you get what you measure and reward,* the choice of waste measures has to be driven by how they affect behavior.

Since there is no such thing as an objective, true, or "real" measure of performance, the goal of the measurement process has to be to choose seven to ten different measures that will motivate people to perform well, to eliminate waste, and to balance their efforts to ensure that the organization and its customers benefit—rather than solely to meet their own personal goals. The objective is not to try to control people or to prevent them from exercising judgments and taking actions in line with their own self-interest, but rather to link individual self-interest to the fate of the organization as a whole. Building a viable future for an organization begins with and depends on "win-win" decisions and solutions to problems that benefit everyone. Eliminating waste from the organization creates the potential for the win-win approach to management. The attainment of this goal is driven by the types of measurements a company has in its portfolio as well as how those measurements are used.

The *use factor* in the measurements arena is seldom discussed. Instead, most companies pursue measurements as though they provide an objective basis for evaluating individuals and keeping the organization on track. When measures are used to control people and their behavior, rather than to motivate them, though, they create dysfunctional consequences. The dysfunctional consequences of measurements have been studied and documented in company after company, situation after situation.[1] There is little question that how measurements are used is the critical element in defining their impact on the organization and its future. Any measure can be used as a hammer, driving people to do what they are told to do. But this coercive use of measurements often degrades performance rather than improves it, as people do only what they are told to do and no more. This is a recipe for disaster in the fast-paced world of business.

Putting the power of each individual to its full use begins with trust, enforced by measurements that help people better understand the potential outcomes of their decisions and actions. Measurements in this setting are tools designed and used by individuals to help them do their jobs better. In this situation, measurements reinforce learning and support growth. The same measure used as a control tool might actually destroy the organization's future value-creating ability. Using measurements to learn and to better understand the organization, rather than to control the actions of people, is the basis for long-term, sustainable success.

Revisiting the Efficiency Mirage

At a Boston-based financial firm, using measurements as control tools was stopped in time to prevent long-term problems. In the pursuit of the Baldrige award for quality and the growth of its market presence, this company began pursuing measurements that would ensure that every call coming in to customer service would be handled promptly. The measurements used were "number of calls answered by the third ring," "number of calls answered by customer service representative," and "time on phone per customer." The goal of these new measurements was to push the representatives to respond quickly to customer requests for service.

As these new measurements began to appear, top management used them to focus attention on service representatives who took too long to deal with any one customer or answered too few calls. Assuming that these individuals were not performing well against customer expectations for speedy answers to their questions, these "malingerers" were increasingly pressured to improve their performance. Increased efficiency was the only performance that mattered. The down results of this approach, detailed in Chapter 3, rapidly appeared.

Most of the customer service representatives accepted the mandate to deal with customers quickly and "efficiently," but one of the company's service superstars continued to perform badly against the new measurements. Despite increasing pressure to improve, this individual continued to do her job the way she felt it should be done. In desperation, the manager of the unit called the woman in to motivate her to meet the performance objectives set for the group. What the manager found out from this representative shed new light on the measurements and their implication for quality customer service.

The service representative's comments were straightforward. "My job is to make sure we please the customer. Sometimes that takes a bit of time as I look up different transactions or deal with errors. But I make sure I fix the problem and give the customer the facts, not hurry them off the phone. These measures don't encourage us to help the customer. They drive us to get them off the phone—quick!" The message embedded in these comments was that serving the customer required answering their questions completely and accurately and not simply picking up the phone. Some queries could be answered quickly to the customer's satisfaction; some could not. This individual's effort to meet customer requirements was not dependent on efficiency; it was driven by effectiveness—doing the right thing.

When the core issue in the company's pursuit of customer satisfaction was identified, it shifted its measurements and objectives to ensure that "quality service" meant solving problems—not shifting or ignoring them to grab the next phone call coming in. Efficiency measures were dropped and were replaced by effectiveness measurements and an ongoing emphasis on doing the right things for the customer, no matter how much effort this might entail.

Measurements that focus solely on efficiency and that are used as tools of control will always trigger some form of dysfunctional behavior. Recognizing this fact, the goal of the measurement process must be to motivate people to perform effectively. Driving people to do things faster does not ensure that they will be done better or cheaper or that the efforts they undertake will yield the desired results. On the other hand, if the measurements focus on eliminating waste and rewarding continuous improvement, they will support an active questioning and modification of existing work to better meet customer requirements. The keys to sustainable growth are motivation and learning—not control.

THE MANY FACES OF WASTE

It's all in the day's work, as the huntsman said when the lion ate him.

CHARLES KINGSLEY (5)

Waste can be found everywhere in an organization. Born of inattention or a frantic drive to get things done, waste consumes a company's profit potential and puts its future at risk. It is a risk that is seldom discussed because it cannot be seen: waste isn't a visible cancer, it is an invisible one. Waste is invisible because it isn't measured, highlighted, or focused on within the normal course of doing business. In the active pursuit of results and new ventures, companies often fail to take the time to ensure that the actions taken every day in the organization make sense and that they support future growth. As the organization drives relentlessly forward and seeks new opportunities, waste creeps in, slowly deflating the energy of the firm and its capability to regenerate itself. The creeping waste invasion grows in the fertile ground of new ideas and old practices.

Designing Waste into an Organization

Mistakes that are made as ideas are transformed into marketable goods and services have a long shelf life. Whether that mistake is in the design of a process, the markets chosen for a product, the manufacturability of a good, or the basic structure of a service, it is a mistake that is difficult to correct (see Chapter 4). The waste created by errors in the design and launch of a product starts long before the first unit is made and continues on through the production process as "re's," excesses, complexity, variation, "un's," and interruptions occur. Ninety percent of the cost and the waste caused by a product is set when it is designed, and this fact is driving many companies to improve how the design process is managed.

One of the most useful tools for helping a company avoid building in excesses to a product is *target costing*. Target costing works backward from the optimal price needed to obtain a desired market share to determine an allowable cost. At Toyota today, no product is launched before its projected cost meets this allowable cost target. Once the product launches, a company has to play catch up to reach its target cost, trying to move up the learning curve fast enough to hit its target and absorb the inevitable downward push of prices as competition emerges in the marketplace.

Target costing helps a company eliminate excess costs before it launches a product. One of the ways this change is achieved is through improvements in the manufacturability of the product as well as the materials used to build it. Another alternative for squeezing cost out of a product is to combat excess complexity in its construction by using standard components wherever possible. The potential for removing cost and waste before a product is put into production is tremendous; once the waste meter has started ticking on the plant floor, shutting it off can be difficult.

Perhaps the greatest waste is the failure to create marketable products with the dollars spent on research and development. 3M has found the secret to unleashing the power of its laboratories into the market. The secret is to back each commercially viable idea with the resources it needs to succeed. It is a strategy that continues to pay off at 3M, which continues to hold the best-in-class designation in this critical area.

Budgeting in Waste

Some waste is built in by design, but other waste is an outgrowth of the way companies budget (see Chapter 5). Capital budgeting is one of the biggest games played in a company. Relying on cash-flow numbers that can be soft, companies run elaborate discounted cash-flow analyses of investment options, choosing those that promise the greatest return. This logical approach to rationing the scarce resources of an organization can build in waste in several different ways. First, if the asset is not added to a bottleneck area of the process (back office or plant), it will not yield the promised benefit but instead will add to the waste already taking place. Second, if the benefits promised by a project are audited to ensure that they come to pass, capital budgeting can become a gentleman's game of liar's poker. This doesn't mean that everyone lies or is out to harm the company, but poor follow-up procedures result in a loss of knowledge that cannot be regained.

Some companies try to avoid part of this game by splitting their capital asset requests into three piles: growth, replacement, and survival. Growth decisions are made to gain a competitive advantage in the future; putting cash-flow numbers on these decisions is difficult at best. The basis for making a survival-based capital-asset decision, on the other hand, is whether a future is wanted at all. These decisions require much more analysis than that possible within a typical payback or discounted cash-flow model. Only replacement decisions have enough certainty surrounding them to support the use of cash-flow-based analysis.

Games played in the annual budgeting process also result in waste. One game—the use of incremental budgets—builds in new forms of waste year after year. Several alternatives to the typical budgeting games (pass the variance, use it or lose it, flavor of the month), such as Stratus Computer's cost-control model built on activity-based budgets and the use of several different sets of measurements to capture budget-based waste, were presented in our discussion of this topic. When budgets build in waste and the culture of the organization drives everyone to "use it or lose it" (the "it" being their piece of the budgeting pie), a company can have a difficult time reaching its profit potential.

The Waste Embedded in Capacity

Another way an organization builds in waste is in the way its capacity is structured and used (see Chapter 6). The assumptions used to build capacity in a plant are usually logical, but over time the incremental addition of new machines and new processes throws the plant out of balance. Excess capacity proliferates, as assets are added to non-bottleneck areas.

Once the resources begin to be used, the many ways in which capacity can be wasted grows. The baseline expectations, or capacity limits, for the system normally build in 20 to 30 percent waste. This defined "practical" capacity is seldom reached, though. In most companies, reaching 80 percent of this number is considered to be acceptable performance. At this point, a company has thrown away 36 percent of its capacity ($.8 \times .8 = .64$ used). But the waste doesn't stop there. The practical capacity number used by most companies is based on a sixteen-hour, five-day clock (eighty hours) rather than a twenty-four-hour, seven-day clock (168 hours). This approach increases the total waste factor to 70 percent ($80/168 \times .64$ use ratio on defined capacity = .30 used in total). When 70 percent of the available capacity is assumed away in a plant, it is difficult to generate profits.

The effective management of capacity is emerging as the key to a company's profit potential. Whether the resources being managed are people or machines, the lessons being learned remain the same: if waste is assumed into a process or an organization in its capacity analysis, it is a deadweight loss to the company that cannot be recovered in the short term. Only by measuring and reporting this form of waste can an organization turn the tide against capacity-based losses.

Accounting and the Language of Waste

The discussion in Chapter 7 examined how waste is created by the way accounting language defines and treats various forms of resources. Assets that generate waste, such as inventory, as well as expenses that are the basis for long-term value creation (research and development, for instance) were looked at. The basic message that emerged was that the way accounting defines its assets, liabilities, and expenses can affect behavior in an organization that runs counter to its best long-term interests.

Building waste measurements and analysis into the language of business will offset many of the problems caused by traditional accounting approaches and can help a company better understand the core features of its value-creating ability. Where accounting is concerned with historical costs and balancing the general ledger, waste measures are focused on ensuring that the value represented by every resource is used to its fullest. Waste measures are actionable. They make visible the lost opportunities for generating profit and long-term competitive advantage. Without waste measures, this information is lost in a smokescreen of accounting transactions, average costs, and variances, never to see the light of day. Accounting isn't bad; it simply isn't the only source of information a company should rely on.

Quality Costs and Waste

The waste created by poor quality procedures and products is not a new topic. In fact, it is a lesson that has been driven home since the entry of Japanese companies into Western markets in the late 1970s. Their success, based on the belief that quality is the essential ingredient for achieving long-term profitability, has debunked the myth that high quality means high cost. Instead, high-quality production and products actually lead to low costs as the waste created by errors is eliminated.

In tracking the cost of quality in Chapter 8, the only expenditures that were not defined as waste are those focused on preventing mistakes from taking place. Preventive costs include training, value analysis, product analysis and design, and any other form of work or expense that focuses on eliminating the potential for error. Costs generated by detecting, fixing, or replacing parts or products that fail to meet quality standards are all waste. The waste created by detecting an error may be less than the waste generated by not detecting it, but it is waste nonetheless. Finally, reworking defective parts may be the biggest waste of all because in addition to the excess cost created by rework, the company loses the opportunity to analyze the defect and learn from it. Quality comes from knowledge and understanding, not solely from tight standards and controls.

Waste in Outsourcing

The final area of waste explored in this book was that created by outsourcing decisions (see Chapter 9). Outsourcing often creates layers of hidden costs and waste as a company trades costs it can see (labor) for costs it can't see (excess freight, delays, and loss of expertise). In many cases, the costs that were to be eliminated by outsourcing are simply shifted to a different part of the organization: avoidable costs aren't avoided in this case. Companies like Lifeline Corporation have begun to reverse their outsourcing decisions as their true costs have surfaced. Outsourcing is not an absolute good.

A second major issue in outsourcing is the danger a company faces when it begins to outsource some or all the activities that make up its core competency. With this insidious form of waste, the company gives away its potential to generate new products or new value in the future for a small cost "savings" today (which may be an illusory saving). Whenever a decision fails to take the long-term profitability and survival of the organization into account due to a single-minded quest for short-term profit improvements, waste is created. Some of the waste may not be visible for years after the decision is made, but it begins to grow the day short-term concerns begin to dominate long-term growth.

MEASURING WASTE: A FRAMEWORK FOR ACTION

Out of action, action of any sort, there grows a peculiar, useful, everyday wisdom. Truth is rarely found by the idle. Nor is it the result of deep and long study. It is a sort of essence that is secreted from a concrete deed.

DR. FRANK CRANE
"Habit," *Essays* (1)

The only useful tool is one that shapes action within an organization. While it is useful to think, analyze, and debate the short- and long-term implications of the many different opportunities and issues confronting the organization, in the end action has to be taken. Waste measures provide a framework for action that ensures that a company will always make the best of the resources it has at its command, turning them to their best use. Waste measures remind everyone that the real tradeoff being made every day is between profit and waste and not between cost and revenue.

Combining the above discussions, a framework for action based on waste measures can be developed (see Figure 10.3). The basic goals underlying this framework are as follows:

- *Completeness* Measurements have to tell the whole story and not just the parts of the events that everyone wants to hear. Any measure that hides information has to be offset by one that reveals it.

- *Objectivity* To support ongoing decision making that builds a company's profit potential, a measure has to be objective. If a cost is not avoided, the measurement has to reveal this. If politics are driving behavior rather than "facts," the measurements have to reveal the effect of these decisions. Measurements have to be objective if they are to serve as the basis for action in organizations.

- *Timeliness* To be actionable, a measure has to be available before decisions are made. Waste measures do not rely on closing accounting ledgers or the ending of a month to be available. They are an ever-present reminder that waste can creep into every activity and every organization.

- *Support learning* Sound actions grow from knowledge about an organization and its value-creating abilities. Waste measures support learning as they pinpoint the waste that can be eliminated through continuous improvement efforts. Waste measures detail the loss of profits that result from decisions and support the active analysis of the tradeoffs inherent in everyday organizational life.

FIGURE 10.3   ELIMINATING WASTE: A FRAMEWORK FOR ACTION

Envision waste.

Learn from waste.

Identify waste wherever it's found.

Measure waste to make it visible.   *Insure*

Investigate every activity for waste.   *Tomorrow*

Negotiate to eliminate waste.

Analyze the causes of waste.

Track waste to prevent its growth.

Eliminate waste wherever it's found.

Actionable measurements make sense to everyone involved, quickly identify problems as they emerge, and honestly and objectively detail the good and bad outcomes of a decision. Actionable measurements have to provide clear, strong signals of where change is needed and why. They have to create an urge to act wherever they appear. To accomplish these goals, actionable measurements have to make visible the invisible events of daily organizational life.

Waste measurements provide a framework for action because they pinpoint errors in processes, assumptions, and activities that limit a company's future value-creating ability. While debates may rage about whether the practical capacity of a plant is 10,000 units a day or 12,000, when the waste created by these assumptions is highlighted, the focus shifts to finding a way to use existing capabilities better. The former debate does not result in action; the latter does. Waste measurements turn theoretical debates into action by revealing opportunities for improvement.

In the final analysis, the goal of any organization has to be to generate the most value possible given the scarce resources it has at its disposal. To achieve this goal, waste has to be constantly squeezed out, wherever it emerges. Waste has to be measured and eliminated constantly because the second it is ignored, waste grows. Waste grows in the assumptions used to frame action, the actions themselves, the interactions between activities along the value chain, and in every decision made within an organization. Keeping the waste monster at bay requires constant attention and a single-minded focus on eliminating waste wherever it appears. "Waste not, want not" is more than a proverb: it's the basic tenet of organizational life in the 1990s and beyond.

No man can say anything of the future. We need not bother about it. The future has always cared for itself in spite of our well-meant efforts to hamper it. If today we do the task we can best do, then we are doing all that we can do.

HENRY FORD
Today and Tomorrow (1926, p. 277)

Notes

Chapter 1

1. Throughout this book, various quotations will be used to introduce sections and summarize points. To make the text less cumbersome, the source for the quotation will be noted as a number in parentheses. The list of titles corresponding to these numbers can be found in the reference section of the book. The only exception to this rule will be when the quote is pulled from an original source, such as Ford's *Today and Tomorrow*. In this case, the full citation will be found in the list of references.

2. Briefly, target costing starts with a derived market price that will ensure a desired market share for a company's product and removes from it the desired profit margin (20 to 25 percent), resulting in a target, or allowable, cost for making a product or providing a service. Projected cost is then compared to this target. If actual exceeds target cost, plans and projects are developed to eliminate this excess cost—or waste—from the product. Most Japanese, and the best-run Western, companies use target costing extensively in the early stages of product and process design.

3. Key works by Williamson are noted in the reference section.

4. From an interview in *USA Today*, February 10, 1994, p. 4B.

5. The "Hawthorne effect" is the name given to the results of a series of experiments conducted at Western Electric in the early 1950s. Researchers found that productivity was enhanced when lighting improvements were made but that over time these improvements disappeared. The explanation for this temporary improvement was simple: line workers improved their performance because someone was paying attention to them; when the attention abated, the improvements abated.

Chapter 2

1. Occam's Razor is the name given to a theory developed by Occam to describe a very basic idea: every idea or approach should be reduced to its simplest terms. There should be no more words, concepts, or relationships than are absolutely necessary to accomplish the task. Reflecting a view first traced to Aristotle, Occam is one of many proponents of the view that simple solutions and simple models perform better—are better snapshots and models of reality—than complex ones.
2. J.P. Womack, D.T. Jones, and D. Roos, *The Machine that Changed the World* (New York: Macmillan Publishing Company, 1990).
3. E. Goldratt and J. Cox, *The Goal: A Process of Continuous Improvement* (Croton-on-Hudson, NY: North River Press, 1986).

Chapter 3

1. This example has been modified to protect any and all actual data as revealed by the company. All the numbers presented are fictitious. Only the situation remains—one where a good company found a way to measure effectiveness and use it to improve its performance against customer expectations.
2. Eastern Candy is a pseudonym for this company, which requested that its name not be used in this example.
3. For further information on the Avon story or on the benchmarking process in general, refer to C. McNair and K. Leibfried, *Benchmarking: Tool for Continuous Improvement* (Essex Junction, VT: Oliver Wight Publications, Omneo, 1992).

Chapter 4

1. *New Webster's Dictionary of the English Language* (New York: Belair Publishing Company, 1981), p. 93.
2. C. Berliner and J. Brimson (eds.), *Cost Management for Today's Advanced Manufacturing: CAM-I Conceptual Design* (Boston: Harvard Business School Press, 1988), pp. 31–32.

3. Dr. Robert Howell is believed to be the first person to use the term *outside-in top-down accounting* as a depiction of target costing. His insights and comments on the subjects covered in this book are greatly appreciated.
4. Berliner and Brimson (1988), pp. 45–47. The list compiled by these authors, as well as personal experiences, form the backdrop for this section.

Chapter 5

1. The complete study is detailed in Kenneth A. Merchant, *Rewarding Performance: Motivating Profit Center Managers* (Boston: Harvard Business School Press, 1989).

Chapter 6

1. Goldratt and Cox (1986), p. 158.

Chapter 10

1. One of the best summary discussions of the dysfunctional consequences of measurement can be found in Ken Merchant's book, *Control in Business Organizations* (Cambridge, MA: Ballinger Publishing, 1985).

References

Books of quotations used throughout the text, per their assigned number:

(1) Edward F. Murphy. *Webster's Treasury of Relevant Quotations*. New York: Greenwich House, 1978.
(2) Dr. Laurence J. Peter. *Peter's Quotations: Ideas for Our Times*. New York: Bantam Books, 1979.
(3) Barbara Ann Kipfer (ed.). *Bartlett's Book of Business Quotations*. Boston: Little, Brown, 1994.
(4) Donald O. Bolander (ed.). *The New Webster's Dictionary of Quotes and Famous Phrases*. New York: Berkley Books, 1991.
(5) Martin H. Manser (ed.). *The Chambers Book of Business Quotations*. Edinburgh: Chambers, 1987.
(6) Caldwell van Roden (ed.). *20/20 Business Thinking*. York, PA: Wellspring, 1987.
(7) Richard A. Moran. *Beware of Those Who Ask for Feedback*. New York: Harper Business, 1994.
(8) Lee Ward Shore. *Mediations for Men Who Do Next to Nothing*. New York: Time Warner Books, 1994.

General References:

Berliner, Callie, and James Brimson (eds.). *Cost Management for Today's Advanced Manufacturing: The CAM-I Conceptual Design*. Boston:. Harvard Business School Press, 1988.

Blanchard, B. S. *Design and Manage to Life Cycle Cost*. Portland, OR: M/A Press, 1978.

Curtis, Donald A. *Management Rediscovered: How Companies Can Escape the Numbers Trap*. Homewood, IL: Business One Irwin, 1990.

Dixon, J.R., Alfred Nanni, and T. Vollmann. *The New Performance Challenge: Measuring Operations for World-Class Competition.* Homewood, IL: Business One Irwin, 1990.

Ford, Henry. *Today and Tomorrow* (reprint edition). Cambridge, MA: Productivity Press, 1988. Original 1926 edition was published by Doubleday, Page.

Goldratt, E., and J. Cox. *The Goal: A Process of Continuous Improvement.* Croton-on-Hudson, NY: North River Press, 1986.

Hall, Robert. *The Soul of the Enterprise: Creating a Dynamic Vision for American Manufacturing.* New York: Harper Business, 1993.

Imai, Masaaki. *Kaizen: The Key to Japan's Competitive Success.* New York: Random House, 1986.

Johnson, H. Thomas. *Relevance Regained: From Top-Down Control to Bottom-Up Empowerment.* New York: Free Press, 1992.

Lynch, Richard, and K. Cross. *Measure Up! Yardsticks for Continuous Improvements.* Cambridge, MA: Basil Blackwell, 1991.

McNair, C., and K. Leibfried. *Benchmarking: Tool for Continuous Improvement.* Essex Junction, VT: Oliver Wight Publications, Omneo, 1992.

Merchant, Kenneth A. *Control in Business Organizations.* Boston: Pitman, 1985.

———. *Rewarding Performance: Motivating Profit Center Managers.* Boston: Harvard Business School Press, 1989.

Riahi-Belkaoui, Ahmed. *Value-Added Reporting: Lessons for the United States.* New York: Quorum, 1992.

Williamson, Oliver E. *Markets and Hierarchies: Analysis and Antitrust Implications.* New York: Free Press, 1985.

———. *Corporate Control and Business Behavior.* Englewood Cliffs, NJ: Prentice-Hall, 1970.

Index

About the Author

Dr. C.J. McNair is the Chandor Professor of Accounting at Babson College in Wellesley, Massachusetts. Since her graduation from Columbia University in 1986, Dr. McNair has done extensive research, writing, teaching, and consulting in the field of management accounting, management control, and integrated performance measurement systems. She is actively involved in creating new measures in businesses around the world, new methods for teaching management accounting, and has completed extensive field research and experiential learning projects during her career. In addition to these professional interests, she enjoys cooking, quilting, reading, and dabbling at golf.